DEMOCRACY IN BLACK

C.1

DEMOCRACY IN BLACK

HOW RACE STILL ENSLAVES THE AMERICAN SOUL

EDDIE S. GLAUDE JR.

CROWN PUBLISHERS

NEW YORK

Library of Congress Cataloging-in-Publication Data
Names: Glaude, Eddie S., Jr., 1968–
Title: Democracy in Black: How Race Still Enslaves
the American Soul / Eddie S. Glaude Jr.
Description: New York: Crown, 2016. | Includes bibliographical references and index.
Identifiers: LCCN 2015028508 | ISBN 9780804137416 (hardback)
Subjects: LCSH: African Americans—Social conditions—21st century. | African
Americans—Economic conditions—21st century. | Racism—United States—
History—21st century. | Race discrimination—United States—History—21st
century. | United States—Race relations—21st century. | BISAC: SOCIAL
SCIENCE / Ethnic Studies / African American Studies. | SOCIAL SCIENCE /
Discrimination & Race Relations. | HISTORY / United States / 21st Century.
Classification: LCC E185.615 .G548 2016 | DDC 305.896/0730905—
dc23 LC record available at lccn.loc.gov/2015028508

ISBN 978-0-8041-3741-6
Ebook ISBN 978-0-8041-3742-3

Printed in the United States of America

Jacket design by Eric White
Jacket photograph: William Moran/GalleryStock

10 9 8 7 6 5 4 3 2 1

First Edition

To Cornel West and Langston Glaude

My inspiration to keep fighting until the last breath

CONTENTS

DEMOCRACY IN BLACK

INTRODUCTION

A THICK FOG OF UNREALITY

M ost of the businesses on West Florissant in Ferguson were boarded up. City officials had informed the owners that the grand jury's decision would be announced within days. They braced themselves for what was to come. To my Mississippi Gulf Coast eyes the town looked like it was preparing for a major hurricane. Plywood was everywhere.

My colleague and I were in Cathy's Kitchen Restaurant & Diner on South Florissant at around 8:30 p.m. waiting to talk with a small group of activists in the Ferguson movement. Apparently this was a favorite late-evening meeting spot for some of the protesters. It was nearing closing time, but the owner, Cathy Jenkins, told us to take our time and order whatever we liked. She and her husband were holding a staff meeting. They were preparing for the grand jury announcement and urging their staff to stay safe. There were no boards on the windows. They didn't expect anything to happen to the restaurant.

Alexis, Brittany, and Ashley finally arrived. These three dynamic young women had emerged as leading voices in the Ferguson movement and were cofounders of Millennial Activists United, a grassroots organization demanding "accountability for victims of social injustice in Ferguson, across America, and the world." Alexis was full of energy.

She walked in the door smiling and talking. Brittany was calm and subdued. She seemed reserved while Ashley brimmed with confidence; she carried herself like a leader. All of them looked like teenagers. Their eyes told you they were older.

Over a plate of sweet-and-spicy wings and fries, we talked about what had happened on August 9, 2014. But, in many ways, the conversation was about how the death of Michael Brown had rescued them from the challenges of daily life. "Every day you wake up, it's a conscious choice to get out your bed and go about your day," said Ashley. "I was waking up every day, and I was like, all right, today I'm going to stay alive. Counting down the hours until I'm going to shoot myself." Alexis and Brittany stared at her as she talked, as if Ashley was describing all of them. "Now it's like, okay, you've got to get up. You can't kill yourself today, because you got to do this. You've got this meeting, you've got to go protest at seven o'clock. You've got to chant. They need somebody up there to chant." Alexis put it bluntly: "Michael Brown saved my life."

Something happened in Ferguson that transformed these young women and transfixed the nation. As one of them said, "You just felt something different in the air." As if the fog was lifting a bit. I couldn't help but think of the contrast. They came of age politically with President Barack Obama in office and now they bathed in the intense rage of Ferguson. In so many ways, these young people were unprecedented.

District Attorney Bob McCulloch announced the grand jury decision not to indict Darren Wilson, the officer who shot and killed Brown, on November 24, 2014. By then I was back in Princeton, watching the press conference with a group of mostly black undergraduates. The students were overcome with emotion. They would later stage an impromptu protest on Prospect Street, where Princeton's tony eating clubs are located. They wanted to disturb the peace.

In Ferguson, tensions reached a fever pitch and the night turned ugly. The conflict spread to South Florissant. Businesses were vandalized and some burned to the ground. A group of young protesters linked arms in front of Cathy's Kitchen and protected it as if it were their own. Something different was definitely in the air.

In his last book, *Where Do We Go from Here: Chaos or Community?*, Dr. Martin Luther King Jr. argued, among other things, that white supremacy stood in the way of democracy in this country, that it was an ever-present force in America frustrating the dreams of the nation's darker citizens and undermining any pretense to racial justice. He wrote:

> *Negroes have proceeded from a premise that equality means what it says, and they have taken white Americans at their word when they talked of it as an objective. But most whites in America . . . proceed from a premise that equality is a* loose expression for improvement. *White America is not even psychologically organized to close the gap—essentially it seeks only to make it less painful and less obvious but in most respects to retain it. (Emphasis added.)*

Matters have not changed much since 1967. Jim Crow laws are no more, and we elected our first black president, but it is still the case, as Dr. King said, that in this country the idea of racial equality remains "a loose expression for improvement." When thought of in this way, racial justice gets reduced to a charitable enterprise—a practice by which white people "do good" for black people. That is not equality. Confronting this fact would take us a long way toward achieving racial justice in this country.

More immediately, confronting this fact would remove our blinders and allow us to see the crisis engulfing black America. The 2008 economic recession devastated black communities across the country. People lost their homes. Life savings disappeared. Thousands found themselves out of work with no prospect of finding another job. This book details what I call the Great Black Depression, and shows how the current rhetoric of economic recovery does not include the majority of black communities in this country.

It challenges the pervasive silence about the crisis in black communities and puts forward an idea of American democracy shorn of its racist baggage. This book offers a thicker description of the current state of black America. It shows how what I call the value gap (the belief that white people are valued more than others) and racial habits (the things we do, without thinking, that sustain the value gap) undergird racial inequality, and how white and black fears block the way to racial justice in this country.

President Obama's election supposedly meant that we had turned a corner. We wanted to believe that we were leaving something bad behind. But we have seen and experienced so much ugliness over these past seven years. How many times have we watched black parents in anguish as they buried their children? As they stood before the press and demanded justice, joined with other parents in a communion of grief? The deaths of Trayvon Martin, Michael Brown, Sandra Bland, and so many others shattered any illusion we might have had about a post-racial America. People from all over the country took to the streets. Ferguson and Baltimore ignited our frustrations. Chants of "Hands up, don't shoot" and "I can't breathe" and "Black lives matter" let the world know that race is far from being a nonissue in this country. Meanwhile, Republicans wrapped the flag around their bigotry and couched it in criticisms of big government. In 2008, Republican presidential nominee Mitt Romney declared that 47 percent of the Americans who voted for Obama were "takers," people "who are dependent upon government, who believe that they are victims, who believe that government has a responsibility to care for them, who believe they are entitled to health care, to food, to housing, to you-name-it." Although he didn't say it explicitly, everyone knew that black people were part of that 47 percent.

Beyond the increase in explicit racism—the loud racists have gotten louder since the 2008 election (it almost feels like some white people have lost their minds)—black people have suffered tremendously on Obama's watch. Black unemployment remains high. Home foreclosures continue. The wealth gap between blacks and whites has grown wider. More young black families and children than ever are drowning in poverty. And police have been on what seems like a rampage—killing young black people at alarming rates. In short, black communities have been devastated. And Obama's most publicized initiative in the face of all this, even as the spate of racial incidents pressured him to be more forthright about this issue, has been My Brother's Keeper, a public-private partnership to address the crisis of young men and boys of color—a Band-Aid for a gunshot wound.

Obama reminds me of Herman Melville's *Confidence Man*: he sees exactly what we want and what we fear and adjusts himself accordingly. And what Melville believed people wanted more than anything was hope, a sense of the possibility of things for themselves and for the world. I am not sure Melville understood, although he might have, the depth of that claim for black folk. For us, hope has always come with a heavy dose of realism. It couldn't be otherwise in a world such as ours, where the color of your skin closes off certain possibilities from the moment you draw your first breath. W. E. B. Du Bois captured it best as "a hope not hopeless but unhopeful"—a blues-soaked sensibility that chastens one's expectations of the world, because the white people in it can be so hateful and mean.

In 2008 and again in 2012, Obama sold black America the snake oil of hope and change. He joined Bill Clinton and Jimmy Carter, other Democratic confidence men who presented themselves as people who would challenge the racial order of things. Clinton even heralded from a place called Hope. But neither Carter nor Clinton changed the racial habits at the heart of the country. In some ways, they reinforced them. Obama promised more. Or at least we thought he did, until he told us that he wasn't the president of black America. Maybe black people believed he represented real change. Maybe we didn't. Maybe we needed the illusion of hope. It doesn't matter. The reality, amid the thick fog of unmet expectations, is that very little has changed in this country. In fact, things have gotten worse.

Obama is not alone in falling short of a real response. Most black liberals (elected and otherwise) have stood silently by as this economic devastation swallowed black America. Afraid to give ammunition to a boisterous ideological right and never wanting to appear disloyal to their own, they have refused to criticize the president. Instead, we have been asked to shift the blame to a recalcitrant Congress or to trust that they are working on our behalf behind closed doors. I want to expose the limits of this view of black politics—the wrongheaded idea that some leader in some back room can represent the interests of black people without any mechanism of accountability. This view of politics undermines the democratic process in black communities.

Democracy in Black calls for a reimagining of black politics and a remaking of American democracy. The two are knotted together. Both begin with local grassroots organizing and movements. We've witnessed this in the protests and demonstrations in Ferguson, in New York, and in other cities around the country and in the Forward Together moral movement in North Carolina. They have helped free our political imaginations from the romance with President Obama that paints him as the fulfillment of our political dreams by calling attention to all the hell breaking loose around us.

In the end, this book exposes the illusion of innocence at the heart of this nation by pointing out the concrete effects of persistent racial inequality. Most Americans see inequality—and the racial habits that give it life—as aberrations, ways we fail to live up to the idea of America. But we're wrong. Inequality and racial habits are part of the American Idea. They are not just a symptom of bad, racist people who fail to live up to pristine ideals. We are, in the end, what we do. And this is the society we have all made. So much so that we can have a black man in the White House and nearly one million black men and women in the Big House.

For much of our national history we have struggled mightily with the issue of race. The evil of slavery shadowed the birth of this country. Precious ideas like "all men are created equal" were congenitally deformed by the idea that some men and women are valued less than others because of the color of their skin. The value gap was baked into one of the foundational principles of this country. That struggle, at least since 1876 (when the nation turned its back on the possibility of a multiracial democracy with the end of Reconstruction), has been a part of who we are as a nation. We wrestle, like Jacob, with the lived contradiction— not between beliefs and practices, but between and within beliefs themselves. Black folk never aspired to be the moral conscience of the nation, even as black leaders shouted it from the rooftops. It only happened to be the case that our actual lives rested in the gap between who America said it was as a democracy and how we actually lived. Our democratic principles do not exist in a space apart from our national commitment to white supremacy. They have always been bound tightly together, sharing bone and tissue.

Something profound has to happen if we are to change course. A revolution of value and a radical democratic awakening may be this country's only hope for salvation. *Democracy in Black* does not begin with pristine principles or with assumptions about our inherent goodness. Rather, its view of democracy emerges out of an unflinching encounter with lynching trees, prison cells, foreclosed homes, young men and women gunned down by police, and other places where "hope unborn had died." It is also grounded in the unimaginable resolve of a people not just to survive in this country but to flourish in spite of it. The current times are dark. The issues are clear. Our choice now, as we leave behind the confidence men and their false hopes, is either to wake up and give everything to "achieve our country" or to remain asleep as America burns.

CHAPTER ONE

THE GREAT BLACK
DEPRESSION

Christine Frazer cried softly. She had been through hell and back and the wounds had not healed. Chris had worked hard all her life. She and her late husband had dreamed big dreams for themselves and their family. They had played by the rules. But when Chris lost her home to foreclosure in 2012 everything changed. Now, at the age of sixty-five, she was out of work and forced to live in a senior facility, her cherished home gone, her health deteriorating, and her dreams shattered.

"Me and my husband had a business for twenty-five years," she said in disbelief. "I raised my daughter in that home. I wasn't a new homeowner. I had been there for eighteen years."

Before the eviction, Chris had lived with her eighty-five-year-old mother, her adult daughter, and her four-year-old grandson in a triplex home in a suburb of Atlanta, Georgia. The upstairs had three bedrooms, two baths, and two big living rooms. There were two separate apartments downstairs. The house sat on a large plot of land, with lots of open space where Chris's dog, Sheeba, could run around. A minister who was a little person had designed the house. "He had been an architect, I guess. And there was not a square room in that house, the way he designed it. That's why I fell in love with it." Within a year of moving into their home, her husband lost his legs because of diabetes and had to use a wheelchair. "But here's the kicker," Chris said. "Since the house had been built for a dwarf, once the ramp was built, he could maneuver in that house just like anybody else because the switches were lower. It was like God sent us there."

But when Chris lost her job in 2009 she struggled to keep making the payments. The house was underwater. She had already paid $240,000 on a home now valued at $40,000. Her mortgage changed hands at least three times in six months. Chris tried everything to prevent foreclosure, but the latest holder of her loan—Investors One Corporation—decided to evict her. President Obama had created a plan to help distressed borrowers, but Chris couldn't take advantage of it; the program required that homeowners be current on their mortgage, and she was not. "But if you're current on your mortgage, you don't need modification," Chris said. The game seemed rigged to protect the mortgage lenders.

Dekalb County sheriffs and deputies arrived in the middle of the night on May 2, 2012, to evict her. "They came in like I was a dope dealer. At three in the morning they drilled a hole in the lock in my front door. They drilled out the lock and just came in my house. It was the most terrifying moment that I can remember in my life. My grandson is six years old, and to this day he does not like police officers, because he remembers. He remembers."

When the police stormed into the house they ordered Chris and her family to get dressed immediately. Then they proceeded to empty the home of a life's worth of memories. It was chaos. For seven hours the police piled Chris's things onto the street. No one could help. The police had cordoned off the area. "They told me to pack up as if I just had a fire at my home and take my immediate possessions. And I had to leave immediately," she remembered. Everything was scattered, without any care, across the lawn. With no place to go, the family slept in the car—except for the family dog. The police made provisions for Sheeba.

"That was the part that I think came out in the eviction. When they came for me at three in the morning, they didn't have a place for me and my family to go, but the animal shelter came because they knew that there were dogs there. They came with a place for my dog."

The sprawling metropolis of Atlanta sat at the epicenter of the housing crisis that shook the foundations of the American economy. Once considered a promised land where good-paying jobs and affordable living offered a real chance for people to fulfill their dreams, by 2012, Atlanta was a wasteland of foreclosed homes and skyrocketing unemployment. In 2007 black unemployment in greater Atlanta was 8.3 percent, but by 2010, that figure had nearly doubled. Chris was among the casualties. According to the Federal Reserve, Atlanta held the dubious distinction of having "the most government-owned foreclosed properties for sale of any large city." The hard reality was undeniable, and Chris was just one example among many: the housing crisis was devastating black Atlanta, and it hardly stopped there. Like an out-of-control wildfire spreading across dry brushland, the crisis engulfed black America.

It wasn't supposed to be like this.

The road to the housing crisis in black America was paved with good intentions, sort of. In June of 2002 President George W. Bush made his way to the pulpit of a quaint African Methodist Episcopal church in Atlanta. "Now, we've got a problem here in America that we have to address," he told the crowd.

Too many American families, too many minorities do not own a home. There is a home ownership gap in America. The difference between Anglo American and African American and Hispanic home ownership is too big. And we've got to focus the attention of this nation to address this.

Bush had come to St. Paul AME to announce his plans for an "ownership society." By 2010, he wanted to increase homeownership among minorities by at least 5.5 million. This required making it easier for low-income buyers to make a down payment; it meant that more affordable housing needed to be available in certain neighborhoods and involved streamlining the home-buying process.

Bush hoped to achieve his goal through a vast network of public-private partnerships. He announced that Fannie Mae and Freddie Mac would "increase their commitment to minority markets by more than $440 billion." Freddie Mac would make it possible for "consumers with poor credit . . . to get a mortgage with an interest rate that automatically goes down after a period of consistent payments"; Fannie Mae would partner with 100 faith-based organizations to improve homeownership education, and organizations like the Enterprise Foundation would help rebuild and rehabilitate urban neighborhoods in partnership with local community groups.

The congregation lavished the president with applause. It was a surreal moment. Here was the president of the United States, the most powerful man in the world—a Republican—stating unequivocally that he was committed to the idea that people of color should own something.

Before delivering the speech, President Bush toured Park Place South, a new development of affordable housing in an area once marked by crime and urban blight. There, he met Darrin West, a black Atlanta police officer who proudly showed off his new home. The president held up West as an example of what was possible with the policies he was promoting. And Bush's initial efforts to increase homeownership among African Americans were indeed quite successful. The rate of black home-ownership rose to 49.1 percent during the height of the housing boom.

But the initiatives President Bush outlined in Atlanta unleashed torrid forces seeking to exploit "emerging markets." According to the Center for Responsible Lending, African Americans were 150 percent more likely to get a high-cost loan with low interest rates that adjusted *upward* after two or three years. From 2007 to 2009, the African American homeownership rate fell by 6 percent (to the lowest level since 1995), a drop more than twice that experienced by any other racial group in the United States. African Americans lost more than 240,000 homes

One of them was Darrin West. He couldn't sell his home, so he gave it back to the bank and simply walked away. The *New York Times* reported that by 2008, "at least 10 percent of [the] 232 homes" in West's Park Place South development had been hit with foreclosure. This pattern played itself out across black America, as billions of dollars disappeared from communities already strapped for resources.

The irony is obvious and biting. So many Americans reveled in the historic significance of Barack Obama's election in 2008. There was a sense of real, exciting possibility, even as the nation confronted the worst economic crisis since the Great Depression. It was a moment of contrasts, of decline but also of possibility—that somehow we were putting the ugliness of our racial past behind us as the country teetered on economic collapse. Uncertainty shadowed national euphoria, and this was especially true for African Americans. Many danced election night away and talked about the fulfillment of the civil rights movement, then woke up to foreclosure notices on their doors.

The foreclosure crisis among African Americans gives a clear sense of the despair and devastation wrought by what can only be called the Great Black Depression. The 2008 recession threatened the economic foundations of the country; over and over again we heard from economists and pundits that the nation had not experienced anything like this since the Great Depression. Venerable financial institutions collapsed. Liquidity froze. Jobs disappeared overnight. The recession cast a dark economic shadow over America.

But in black America, the reality was even bleaker. I mean this beyond the familiar platitude that says "whenever white America has a cold, black America has the flu." The reality is that by every relevant statistical measure (employment, wages, wealth, etc.) black America has experienced and is experiencing a depression. This is more like the symptoms of a national congenital disease than the flu.

To be sure, the circumstances of black America have waxed and waned since the heyday of the civil rights movement. The black freedom struggle of the 1960s brought unprecedented improvement in the lives of most African Americans. But even with these gains, the gap between whites and blacks persisted through the 1970s and 1980s alongside brewing racial tensions (often because of police violence) and deepening class divisions within black America. Combined with cyclical economic booms and busts, the slow march from the end of Jim Crow to full equality felt more like a bad roller-coaster ride. It was not until the long recovery of the 1990s, spurred by governmental policy and strong economic growth, that we began to see significant economic improvements for black America—particularly for the black middle class.

Fast-forward to the Great Black Depression of 2008. Much of the gains of the 1990s were erased. African Americans lost 31 percent of their wealth between 2007 and 2010. White Americans lost 11 percent. By 2009, 35 percent of African American households had zero or negative net worth. According to the Pew Research Center, by 2011, black families had lost 53 percent of their wealth. Just think about it: an entire decade of economic gains wiped away. Gone. This wasn't just the loss of homes—the primary source of wealth for most African Americans— but lost retirement savings, which shrank by 35 percent from 2007 to 2010. As many struggled to save their homes, as they witnessed the stock market spiral downward and their pensions dwindle to nothing, they took out what little money they had invested in order to keep themselves afloat. Many could not wait for the market to rebound to reap its benefits. Their children won't be able to either.

As they lost their homes and saw their savings wiped out, people also lost their jobs, making it hard to imagine ever clawing their way back to where they'd once been. Often the last hired and first fired, people saw black unemployment soar as a result of the economic collapse. So much so that by November 2010, national black unemployment reached the stunning level of 16 percent (and this figure does not include those who simply dropped out of the labor market). White unemployment stood at 9 percent. Some cities, including Detroit and New York, reported unemployment among black males at close to 50 percent.

For all these reasons, poverty is growing in black America. One out of four African Americans lives in poverty today. One out of three black children grows up in poverty, while only one out of ten white children lives in poverty. One out of five black children is growing up in extreme poverty. That child's parents make less than $11,746 a year for a family of four. They live on $979 a month, $226 a week, or what ends up being $32 a day. In twenty-five of the fifty states and in the District of Columbia, at least 40 percent of African American children are poor. This is galling for a nation that considers itself the leader of the free world and a pioneer of democratic principles.

Given the impact on African American children, this crisis is not only an event of the present. Its implications for future generations of African Americans have yet to be calculated. Chris Frazer's six-year-old grandson will remember the horror of police tossing his family's possessions out in the yard like garbage as they were evicted, but beyond those memories, what will he inherit? Like so many young African Americans in this country, he will have to start economically with little or no help from the previous generation, because social and systemic barriers have severely limited economic mobility for black folk; the Great Black

Depression took the one thing his grandmother could claim as her own. His financial inheritance will be a balance of broken promises.

Such crushing poverty dashes the dreams of millions of children daily. But not only that: it almost ensures that they will lead less healthy lives as they grow up; that they will more than likely drop out of high school; that they will experience some form of violence in their lifetime; that they will likely find themselves caught up in the criminal justice system; and that they will end up raising their children in the same horrifying conditions they grew up in. In short, the terrible effects of the Great Black Depression guarantee, unless we fully understand the urgency of now, that even darker days are ahead.

The very foundations of black America have cracked under the weight of the economic fallout. It has affected what we own, how we work, and the future of our children. But what's really scary is how little anyone outside black America seems to care.

Patricia Hill was defiant. A judge had given her 75 days to vacate her beautiful home in the historic Bronzeville section of Chicago. In 2003 she'd obtained a lower fixed-rate mortgage with the intent of using the savings for extensive home repairs. Five years later Patricia noticed that her mortgage payment had increased by $500. "Can't nobody afford $500 extra a month," she complained. Saxon Mortgage Services said it would correct the mistake. She continued to pay her regular mortgage, only to be told later that her account was in arrears. Patricia was caught in the spider's web of predatory lending.

Eventually the Bank of New York Mellon sold the house right out from under her—"sold it to itself for about a third of its 2010 appraised value," Patricia said. On court order, the police attempted to evict her in 2011, but more than one hundred supporters from the Chicago Anti-Eviction Campaign blocked their efforts. In 2012, on her sixty-first birthday, she was finally evicted. But when we talked about what happened to her, she remained defiant. In fact, Patricia was in her home. The bank still owned the property. But she says she never stopped living in the house.

"I never stopped receiving my mail here. I never stopped paying my homeowner's insurance. I never stopped paying my utilities. They won't allow me to pay my mortgage. Fine. They won't allow me to pay taxes. Fine. So everything has been as if I was here anyway, because I was." As she put it, "This is my reparation."

Patricia's home is a vintage two-story Greystone built in 1888. It has a front facade made of Bedford limestone, a distinctive feature of this architectural style. When she describes her home, her voice dances with pride. "Let's see, you have twelve-foot ceilings. You have the very high doors entering into the home and the foyer." A large stairway leads upstairs, with woodwork along the walls. "These little panels in the hallways, going up the stairs, around—I don't even know how to describe it." She has three open fireplaces and a restored cottage in the back.

"When I came back I was surprised, you know, the first night here: Oh, I can hear crickets again. . . . I look right outside my window and, you know, I can see the garden, and this is really where I thought I was going to live out the rest of my life. . . . This was my intent. I had no idea. None. I made everything secure. You know, I was paying my bills. I said, 'Okay, I can do this.' This is not an assumable mortgage. This wasn't a HUD. This was a conventional loan. Nothing is going to change." Her voice was no longer dancing.

Patricia said that her foreclosure was just a symptom of a deeper sickness in America: that the country had been sold to foreigners; that corporations, or what she called "corruptorations," and "the banksters" had turned people into commodities; and that black people had become too comfortable with the status quo. "In the late '70s, early '80s, people started getting into 'Oh, well, I want to become more a part of the system.' Because to get you to buy into the system, the system was opening up certain things to make you feel more vested. And when you're vested in something, you're not going to fight against it."

Underneath it all, even as she railed against the system, Patricia still struggled with the fact that she had lost her home. She had raised three children. She had purchased her first home when she was twenty-six years old. And now, at the age of sixty-three, after a life of public service as a police officer and a teacher, she was a squatter in the home where she had imagined she would spend her last days.

Claims that the recession is over, made in the face of all I have described to this point, only confirm that much of what happens in black America is not a matter of national concern—unless, of course, it threatens people who "really matter." Such a lesson is a hard one to learn in the twenty-first century. We're supposed to be better than this. But we are rearing a generation of black children, as we have done for so many previous generations, to believe that their lives, unlike others who have money, aren't worth as much. This is the price of invisibility.

Inept public institutions in many black communities reinforce the belief that certain populations, certain black people, are disposable— that black lives don't matter. Here we find constellations of public dysfunction dotting the landscape: poor health care delivery (even with Obamacare), neighborhoods without supermarkets or other access to fresh foods, few job opportunities, and payday loan centers that prey on people who need money. As if that isn't enough, public schools repeatedly fail, and black children suffer disproportionately because of it. We see high dropout rates. And local municipalities ruthlessly close budget deficits on the backs of schools servicing these communities. In 2013, Chicago closed nearly 50 schools primarily in poor black and brown neighborhoods. From 2003 to 2013, Detroit closed 150 schools. All the while the police do what society demands: they arrest and lock up black people in these communities at alarming rates. Today they lock up more black people than South Africa did at the height of apartheid.

Many of these communities are *opportunity deserts,* places of tremendous hardship, joblessness, and what seems to be permanent marginalization. Opportunity deserts are those communities, both urban and rural, that lack the resources and public institutions that give those who live there a chance to reach beyond their current lives. They are characterized, in part, by (1) the absence of social networks that point out pathways for professional and educational advance and (2) heightened police surveillance that increases the likelihood of someone's landing in the criminal justice system. Even the most resourceful people here find themselves awash in what the Nigerian novelist Chimamanda Ngozi Adichie calls "the oppressive lethargy of choicelessness," in which people either look somewhere else for opportunity or succumb to the inevitable limits of where they were born. Opportunity deserts are isolated places for disposable people.

This is not to say these communities are without hope, but these are the harsh conditions under which hope dares to blossom. Opportunity deserts are the racial underside of a society that has turned its back on poor people, especially poor black people. This indifference to the poor allows most white Americans to be willfully ignorant of what happens in such places and to ignore the history of racism in this country that has consigned so many black people to poverty with little to no chance of escaping it. Most white Americans never go there— literally or metaphorically—and have a hard time imagining that such places exist.

The result has been the privatization of black misery. Whatever bad things are happening in opportunity deserts, it is not the concern of the state or of Americans who don't live there, beyond questions of their own safety and protection. They see it as an issue of individual behavior and bad choices. People who live in opportunity deserts, Americans think, have done something to deserve to be there. Social misery, understood in this sense, is a private affair. Somehow, people absurdly believe—and they have done so for much of our history— that black social misery is the result of hundreds of thousands of unrelated bad individual decisions by black people all across this country.

Today long-term unemployment among African Americans is at its highest in twenty years and has left many isolated in concentrated poverty while middle-class African Americans face the threat of downward mobility. People are losing their livelihoods and their communities, but little if anything is being said about either. Here the feeling that black people are disposable becomes concrete.

We should be better than this. But it seems that no matter what we do or what happens to us, African Americans can be seen only in a certain way or at certain times. Either our suffering has to be invisible, or that suffering has to be entirely familiar. Somebody has to call us a nigger, or someone has to shoot down an innocent twelve-year-old child, or someone has to massacre nine black people in a church to remind us of the ugliness of our past and present. Otherwise, the nation is unconcerned with the problems of black America, ignoring the dimming eyes of black children waiting to be warehoused in the nation's prisons.

Our segregated lives and our deep fears keep the problems of black folk from coming into full view. And even while hidden, the devastation spreads like cancer. This is the way we deal with race matters in this country: willful blindness. Any other approach threatens our national sense of morality.

The housing market in Atlanta has finally started to recover. Home prices are rising. As of August 2014, in places like Dunwoody, Georgia, northeast of downtown Atlanta, only 12.3 percent of the homes were underwater. But a radically different picture emerged just a short drive south from Dunwoody. In Riverdale, a lower-income community that is 80 percent African American, 76 percent of the mortgages owed on homes exceeded their market value. The so-called recovery hadn't touched many of the African American neighborhoods in metro Atlanta. It is a tale of two cities. Affluent white neighborhoods have bounced back. Moderate-income black communities are still drowning. In fact, nineteen of the thirty ZIP codes with the highest percentage of underwater homes in the country are in metro Atlanta. One of them is Forest Park, Georgia, where Christine Frazer now lives.

After the foreclosure on her home, Chris and her family moved to a trailer, but their trouble didn't stop there. Soon she was diagnosed with an autoimmune disease that leads to muscle weakness and fatigue. "I woke up one morning and one eye was one way and my other eye was the other way," she remembered. "I went to the doctors by the grace of God. I was diagnosed with what they call myasthenia gravis, which is usually brought on by too much stress. I had to start taking steroids and some other kind of medication. Now I take eight medications." Chris doesn't live in the trailer anymore. She moved to a senior living facility in Forest Park. Her daughter lived in Riverdale, but has since moved in with her. The rental market has been brutal.

It is unimaginable for Chris and her family to talk of anything approximating a recovery. They live amid the ruins of their lives, and it takes a tremendous toll. "The aftereffects, not just the housing issue, ruined my health," she said. "They say don't let it stress you out. But what else are you supposed to do? The home that you had for almost twenty years was snatched from you and you couldn't do anything about it, and you're out on the street."

Chris felt invisible, like her life did not and does not matter. She's not alone—millions of black Americans experience these same hardships and the same feelings of invisibility. Our national refusal to acknowledge the Great Black Depression says to black America that the suffering it is enduring is unimportant. It is the latest instance of the contradiction that has defined this country since its birth: our claims to democracy have always been shadowed by the belief that some people—white people—are valued more than others.

CHAPTER TWO

THE VALUE GAP

A merican apathy or willful ignorance toward the suffering caused by the Great Black Depression is disheartening but not surprising. It is simply another manifestation of how little black people are valued in this country.

If the blind eye turned toward black economic suffering doesn't put a fine enough point on that fact, events involving police violence certainly have. When Michael Brown, the eighteen-year-old teenager killed by Darren Wilson of the Ferguson, Missouri, police department, was left dead in the street for four and a half hours with gunshot wounds to the head and body, members of that community saw clearly and felt painfully the undeniable fact that they were valued less. This horrific incident amplified their lived experience. Daily assaults on their humanity by police. Inadequate schools. Crippling unemployment and poverty. Injustices that were all plainly obvious but completely ignored. Now the body of one of their own lay dead for all to see. Think of the irreparable harm done to the psyches of the children in the Canfield Green apartments who saw him in the street.

What became immediately clear when the case hit the news was that the police and much of the nation refused to see Michael Brown. He was the thug who was "no angel," who listened to hip-hop, smoked weed, and stole Swisher Sweets cigarillos. Michael Brown, no matter what his mother said about him and his ambitions, was swallowed by all the ugly stereotypes about young black men. He was not a straight-A student; his life didn't seem promising—so he alone was culpable in his death. He was disposable.

Police actions and community responses in Ferguson and elsewhere increasingly expose a painful reality: the United States remains a nation fundamentally shaped by its racist past and present. This is a hard fact for some Americans to accept. Of course, we are not the same country we were in 1860 or even 1960. Slavery is roundly seen as evil, and legal segregation is ostensibly gone. Black people run Fortune 500 companies; they are mayors of cities and professors at Ivy League schools. But despite the real gains we have made, white supremacy continues to shape this country.

The phrase *white supremacy* conjures images of bad men in hooded robes who believe in white power, burn crosses, and scream the word *nigger*. But that's not quite what I mean here. On a broader level, white supremacy involves the way a society organizes itself, and what and whom it chooses to value. Apartheid in South Africa, the Jim Crow South, and Nazi Germany are clear examples of societies organized by white supremacy. In each case, the belief that white people are valued more than nonwhite people shaped every aspect of social and political life. It determined where you lived, which schools you attended, and what jobs were available to you. It reminded you daily of your status and station in life. And that's white supremacy without all the bluster: a set of practices informed by the fundamental belief that white people are valued more than others.

America isn't exactly like the extreme examples of Nazi Germany or apartheid South Africa, but we do live in a country where, every day, black people confront the damning reality that we are less valued. The data are crystal clear. African Americans suffer chronic double-digit unemployment. We lead the nation in rates of heart disease, cancer, HIV/AIDS. Nearly 1 million of the 2.4 million Americans in prison are black. When we think about the differences between whites and blacks in high school and college graduation rates, in mortality rates, in access to health care, in levels of wealth, in salary differences with comparable education, in the childhood poverty rate, we can see that in this country, white people, particularly those with money, matter more than others. It has been this way since the very day this country was founded.

The crisis currently engulfing black America and the country's indifference to the devastation it has wrought illustrate what I call *the value gap*. We talk about the achievement gap in education or the wealth gap between white Americans and other groups, but the value gap reflects something more basic: that no matter our stated principles or how much progress we think we've made, white people are valued more than others in this country, and that fact continues to shape the life chances of millions of Americans. The value gap is in our national DNA.

At every crucial moment in our nation's history, when there have been fundamental changes in how we've dealt with race, white people asserted the value gap and limited the scope of change. The powerful ideals of the American Revolution, which challenged the authority of monarchs and insisted on the principles of freedom and equality in the context of democratic institutions, were reconciled with the institution of racial slavery. People could talk of freedom and liberty *and* hold black slaves. Even the first immigration and naturalization act, in 1790, allowed only "white persons" to attain citizenship, and that racial understanding of citizenship persisted until 1954. The brutal war to end slavery and the efforts during Reconstruction to imagine a genuine multiracial democracy were tossed aside: Jim Crow took over the South, white supremacy shaped our foreign policy in places like the Philippines and Cuba, and convict leasing emerged as another form of slavery. Cries for "law and order" and of "reverse racism" echoed throughout the nation as black folk marched in the streets, organized in their communities, and forced the government to end Jim Crow and to embrace, at least in principle, the idea of full racial equality. And here we are today: the historic election of our first black president occasioned the vitriol of the Tea Party, urgent efforts to change voting laws in ways that threaten black voters, and the worry that whites are fast becoming a "politically incorrect minority."

Each of these moments of racial progress represents a profound change in the country. America was and is truly different because these events happened. But the extent of the change was always limited by the underlying belief in the supremacy of white people—a belief that adjusted and adapted to new conditions. Niggers became Negroes. Blatant racism became demands for states' rights, and whites became one ethnic group among many. Black people were now dependent on government handouts and affirmative action, lacking individual initiative and self-reliance. Mass incarceration became the answer to calls for law and order. With each step forward, equally powerful forces pulled the nation back in the direction of the status quo. This is what I think people mean when they say little has changed in America with regard to race.

THE AMERICAN IDEA

Americans like to believe that we live in a special country: that the American Revolution introduced democracy to the modern world and that we are free to pursue our dreams in a religiously tolerant society without the burden of rigid class distinctions. In the United States, people can worship wherever they want to, or they can choose not to believe in God at all. Lords and knights don't exist here. And poor people, if they work hard, can escape poverty and even become rich. The amazing bounty of our lands and natural resources also set us apart. It's as if God placed his hands only on us. As patriots of the revolution put it, "With the Revolution, God has shown that THE UNITED STATES OF AMERICA are his vineyard—the principal seat of [His] glorious kingdom." In this view, America is an exceptional place, a chosen nation charged to redeem the world.

Believing this requires that we ignore our history. Even as America was imagined as a New Israel, many black people saw it as Egypt—a "democracy" with black slaves. With the abolition of slavery, black people found themselves relegated to second-class status as the country continued to exploit their labor. Over and over again, the American Idea—that ours was a nation committed to liberty, freedom, and the unfettered pursuit of individual dreams—ran up against the stark reality that black people were valued less than others and that our society was organized to reflect that fact.

Now, those who believe in the American Idea see this as a basic contradiction between our ideals and practices, but not as fundamental to who we are as a nation. We have a Constitution and a set of principles that crystallizes our values and provides whatever possible remedies for people who suffer from racial discrimination. And when we fall short of those principles, Americans will do the work to bridge the gap between our ideals and practices. Our history, so the argument goes, is replete with examples of righting the wrongs of our racist past. The fact that racial inequality persists only suggests that we still have work to do.

But the value gap isn't about the distance between our ideals and practices or whether the United States should be seen as the "Redeemer Nation." It is about the beliefs that inform and shape the principles we claim as uniquely our own—the soil within which all of this stuff grows. If you believe that white people matter more than black people, then the principles of freedom, liberty, and equality—democracy itself—will be distorted and disfigured. If the American Idea shapes our democracy, and that idea is in turn informed by the value gap, then it hardly matters what form our laws and politics take. They may create a framework for equality, but the value gap will always rig the outcomes. We can do the work. In fact, we've done some of the work, and it has cost a great deal to do so. But the value gap at the heart of the American Idea ensures that no matter the form of our system, it will always produce the same results: racial inequality. We can even elect a black president and that inequality would not fundamentally change. Remedying the problem of racial inequality in this country, then, involves ridding ourselves of the value gap.

The problem lies, at least in part, in seeing America as something in the abstract, as an idea separate from our practices. We often frame unjust practices as aberrations that don't live up to what we want America to be. But it's hard to buy that logic when for more than seventy-five years the country's very Constitution dictated that a slave should be counted as three-fifths of a person. Really, what's an ideal when you can't even get it into the founding document? The American Idea has never been quite the pristine paradigm we make it out to be, and it is our inability to acknowledge this fact that nourishes the value gap.

This is no less true today. When Representative Paul Ryan of Wisconsin, for example, talks of the American Idea it feels wholly disconnected from the actual history of this country. For him, the American Idea "describes a way of life made possible by our commitment to the principles of freedom and equality—rooted in our respect for every person's natural rights." He understands it philosophically in the way we think about opportunity and the American dream. In cultural and human terms, Ryan says, the American Idea is manifested in the way we imagine our relationships with the state, with family and civil society, and in virtuous citizenship. Economically, the American Idea is "the belief that broadly shared prosperity is best achieved by allowing individual creativity and ingenuity to emerge and evolve." And this requires free choice and enterprise.

Ryan's hometown of Janesville, Wisconsin, concretized the American Idea for him. There, he came to learn the power of opportunity and hard work. People dreamed dreams and worked their behinds off to achieve them. Even if they faced setbacks and challenges they picked themselves up and, with the help of others in the community, tried again. For him, Janesville represents the values of the American Idea: a tight-knit community where money and class aren't really talked about, where people "make their own opportunities" and share a set of values such as personal responsibility and accountability. Janesville also embraces an idea of a government that doesn't disrupt how we live our lives, but instead protects the spaces for individual innovation and creativity. In small towns like Janesville, government doesn't get in the way. Government keeps us safe, enables fair competition, and provides "some basic protections to the vulnerable from the worst risks of modern life."

I grew up in a small town too, not in Wisconsin, but on the coast of Mississippi. But my hometown, Moss Point, doesn't look much like what Ryan talks about. Of course, people dreamed dreams and worked their behinds off. But their job security waxed and waned with local industry. One day the shipyard was hiring. The next day it was laying people off. Money and class mattered. The town was more than 70 percent black. The local schools struggled, and black unemployment was terribly high. Everything about my childhood let me know that I had to work twice as hard for opportunity and that I shouldn't expect the world to be fair, because the world isn't fair to black people. Here the American Idea wasn't neat and tidy.

My hometown is no less American than his, yet Ryan's American Idea cannot quite countenance the existence of it. His view of the American Idea is unsullied by our racial history and practices; it is set apart from how we actually live our lives. (He even ignores the fact that members of his own community formed a Ku Klux Klan chapter.) And when I say *we*, I don't just mean African Americans. The attitudes of Ryan and his white neighbors in Janesville are just as surely shaped by the value gap as are those of my black neighbors in Moss Point. "I know a lot of people who have a lot of prejudice," Pam O'Leary, the owner of a diner in Janesville, said. "They'll say they're not prejudiced . . . but they'll use certain terms for certain groups." This is America, whether Ryan's American Idea admits it or not.

When I teach Introduction to African American Studies at Princeton I always begin with a quotation from Alexis de Tocqueville's 1835 classic, *Democracy in America.* My hope is to shake the students from the belief that the course is only about black people. I want them to see that when we read about slavery, black religion, blues, jazz, the civil rights movement, and Black Power, these events and moments force us to confront the most difficult questions about American democracy.

Tocqueville helps me lay out the stakes. At the beginning of chapter 10 on the three races, he writes: "I have now finished the main task that I set myself and have, to the best of my ability, described the laws and mores of American democracy." His writing about race comes as an afterthought, as something wholly apart from the issue of American democracy. Tocqueville makes a mistake.

His talk of the *habits of the heart*—what he takes to be the cultural values and assumptions that make us who we are (the values, like individual initiative, that Paul Ryan talks about in Janesville, Wisconsin)— includes assumptions about the value of white people and black people that limit how we think about democracy in this country. White people, particularly propertied white men, actively participated in the political process in the 1830s and 1840s. Black people were either slaves or relegated to the margins of society. That position was justified by a host of beliefs about black people's capacities for self-governance that shaped the daily lives of white Americans. Black people were meant to be servile; everything about our society reflected that fact. To talk of habits of the heart apart from the racial views of Americans is to miss completely one of the crucial blind spots of American democracy at the time. (Unless, of course, you too believed that white people mattered more than black people.) Tocqueville's mistake, I tell my students, is our mistake. Americans often speak of freedom while giving little care to the great legacy of unfreedom at the heart of the American project. We continue to keep separate the American Idea and white supremacy.

Think about it this way. When Communists declare that Stalinism wasn't really communism or when Christians and Muslims say that the horrific things some Christians and Muslims have done in the name of their religion isn't really Christianity or Islam, what are they doing? They are protecting their ideology or the religion from the terrible things that occur in its name. They claim only the good stuff. What gets lost in all of this is that the bad stuff may very well tell us something important about communism, Christianity, or Islam—that there may be something in the ideology and in the traditions themselves that gives rise to the ugly and horrific things some people do in its name. (Minimally, it shows us that these traditions are hotly fought over and never that stable to begin with.)

The same holds true for the American Idea. We like to keep separate the evils of our national past from the sacredness of our ideals. That separation allows us to maintain a pristine idea of America despite all of the ugly things we have done. Americans can celebrate the founding fathers even when we hear John Adams declare to King George, "We will not be your negroes" or learn that Thomas Jefferson wasn't so consistent in his defense of freedom. We keep treating America like we have a great blueprint and we've just strayed from it. But the fact is that we've built the country true. Black folk were never meant to be full-fledged participants in this society. The ideas of freedom and equality, of liberty and citizenship did not apply to us, precisely because we were black. Hell, the ability to vote for the majority of black people wasn't guaranteed until 1965. The value gap limited explicitly the scope and range of democratic life in this country. So when folks claim that American democracy stands apart from white supremacy, they are either lying or they have simply stuck their head in the sand.

Let's be clear. American democracy isn't just a set of abstract principles. Democracy acquires its power and substantive meaning in our living together, with all of its contradictions, its horrors and joys. Black people have shared in that life from the beginning. We have toiled on plantations and in factories. We have worked in homes, nursed babies, washed clothes, and shined shoes. Our lives, despite the circumstances, answered Ralph Waldo Emerson's call to "sing America."

We have also buried our dead here. Cut them down from lynching trees. Identified them as they were discovered floating in rivers, left in alleys to rot after sexual assault, or shot down by a police officer's gun. We have done all this in light of America's most elaborated contradiction: that no matter our stated commitments to democracy, white people in the country where I live are valued more than black people.

When we understand American democracy and white supremacy as inextricably connected we can see how tortuous our efforts have been to accommodate the value gap. For much of our history we have reconciled the contradiction by excluding black people from full participation in American life and creating odd categories to account for them that placed them at the margins of society—categories like "three-fifths of a person" in the Constitution and the doctrine of "separate but equal." With emancipation and the political enfranchisement of black Americans, we invoked the idea of "a more perfect union."

Correction of past wrongdoings, like ending slavery and dismantling legal segregation, confirmed the rightness of our ideals. Nothing fundamental about those ideals needed to change. We simply had to be better people.

I want no part of that story. It blinds us to how the value gap has been so fundamental to who we are as a nation. Over and over again, we have confronted the overriding belief, held by our government and exhibited in our daily lives, in white supremacy. The story blinds most white Americans to the harsh reality of this country. It hems them in. They see only what they want to see. But if we reckon with what has happened and is actually happening in this country, like the Great Black Depression, we can rid ourselves of the dangerous idea that Americans are inherently good or exceptional, and that these sorts of events are aberrations. We can finally leave behind this false idea that the true problem in this country is the gap between our ideals and practices. No. The true problem is our repeated failure to value *all* Americans. As James Baldwin writes:

> *The American Negro has the great advantage of having never believed that collection of myths to which white Americans cling: that their ancestors were all freedom-loving heroes, that they were born in the greatest country the world has ever seen, or that Americans are invincible in battle and wise in peace, that Americans have always dealt honorably with Mexicans and Indians and all other neighbors or inferiors, that American men are the world's most direct and virile, that American women are pure. Negroes know far more about white Americans than that.*

The task at hand is not about securing the goodness of the American Idea or about perfecting the union. It is about according dignity and standing to all Americans no matter the color of their skin.

THE "PROBLEM WITH BLACK PEOPLE"

Today most of us find it difficult to acknowledge the persistence of racial inequality, let alone something like the value gap. And if you reject the claim that white supremacy still shapes this country, there are only two ways to reconcile what's happening across America. Either you point to the passage of civil rights legislation or to a black man's presence in the White House and declare our race problem solved, or you decide that black people must be at fault for their own terrible condition.

Throughout American history, as we have struggled with the issue of race, the particular circumstances of black lives have been hidden by the illusion that white America has adequately addressed "the Negro problem." We have a long history of prematurely proclaiming that our race problems are long over. In the years following the Civil War and Reconstruction, for example, many white Americans lauded the end of the race problem in the country just as Jim Crow took shape in the South. The Supreme Court in the civil rights cases of 1883 declared the Civil Rights Act of 1875 unconstitutional. That law had fined private business owners for engaging in racial discrimination. Many saw the law as an infringement on freedom of choice (Senator Rand Paul made a similar argument in 2011 against the Civil Rights Act of 1964). Slavery had been over for almost twenty years, and the justices cautioned that black people needed to finally stand on their own without the help of government despite crippling poverty, daily violence, and the ascendance of Jim Crow. Justice Joseph P. Bradley wrote the majority opinion.

When a man has emerged from slavery, and, by the aid of beneficent legislation, has shaken off the inseparable concomitants of that state, there must be some stage in the progress of his elevation when he takes the rank of a mere citizen and ceases to be the special

favorite of the laws, and when his rights as a citizen or a man are
to be protected in the ordinary modes by which other men's rights
are protected.

The fact that black people were subject to continued racial discrimination did not warrant unique consideration, according to the Court. The issue of slavery had been settled. Neither the Thirteenth nor the Fourteenth Amendment gave Congress the power to restrict racial discrimination in the private sector. Black people were now like everyone else. Tragically, more than 2,000 black people were lynched in the United States between 1882 and 1903. Didn't matter: the problem had been solved.

Fast-forward to 2013. The Supreme Court struck down a key provision in the Voting Rights Act of 1965. The Court held that Section Four, which determined which states must receive clearance before making any changes to voting procedures, was unconstitutional. Chief Justice John Roberts was clear about the reasoning of the majority. "Our country has changed," he wrote. "[T]he conditions that originally justified the measures no longer characterize voting in the covered jurisdictions." The Court was claiming that the problem the Voting Rights Act sought to resolve was, for the most part, settled. Meanwhile, state after state, many in the covered jurisdictions, passed restrictive voter-identification laws that disproportionately affected black voters.

The illusion that we've solved our race problem often leads to harsh judgments about black people: continued demands for racial equality amount to acts of extortion by people who don't want to take responsibility for themselves. Since the 1980s and the advent of the Reagan revolution, the majority of Americans tend to see racial inequality, if they acknowledge it exists at all, as the fault of black people. Too many black folk have failed to take advantage of the successes of the civil rights movement, the argument goes. They have relied on government handouts that deepened their dependency, and they have failed to hold themselves accountable and responsible for their own circumstances and actions. Bill O'Reilly and many other Republicans argue repeatedly that what's really wrong with the black community isn't racism. It's the breakdown of the family, the absence of fathers, and the failure to embrace education.

Sadly, none of this is new. Throughout this country's history various justifications for the status of black Americans have been put forward. Black people were incapable of civilization, prone to crime, lacking in intelligence, generally lazy, and sexually promiscuous. The list goes on and on. These stereotypes stood in the place of actual black people, and popular culture reinforced them. Americans absorbed these images of black people with characters like Stepin Fetchit and shows like *Amos 'n' Andy*. Today we see similar images on *Cops* or with shows like *Love & Hip Hop*.

Perhaps, then, it's unsurprising that poll data consistently show that many white Americans continue to rate black people as lazier than whites and more likely to prefer to live off of welfare. Even though they are not loud racists, many white Americans associate negative qualities with black people, and that association affects how black individuals are seen and treated, and how policy to remedy racial inequality is imagined. Bill O'Reilly again comes to mind here.

But, as the data show, right-wingers like O'Reilly and the people at Fox News are not alone in their beliefs. In a 2013 NBC News/*Wall Street Journal* poll respondents were asked what they thought was most responsible for the continuing problem of poverty in this country. They were given a list of eight factors, including "too much welfare that prevents initiative," "lack of job opportunities," and "racial discrimination." The last choice revealed how poverty is often associated with black people. Twenty-four percent of the respondents chose "too much government welfare that prevents initiative," making it the most popular answer.

To my mind, this doesn't mean that Americans are mean-spirited people who lack empathy for the less fortunate (although the likes of Paul Ryan and Ted Cruz may make me change my mind). Instead, it shows how we see poverty today. If financial success is primarily understood in terms of individual initiative and ambition, then poverty must be its exact opposite. By that logic, federal programs to benefit the poor, like welfare, won't solve the problem. They will only make it worse.

But this argument seems to apply only when the face of poverty is black. From the New Deal up to Robert Kennedy's tour of Appalachia in 1968, welfare was widely seen as good government. Racist southern populists initially supported the New Deal, because the policies helped the white poor in the region—policies systematically denied to black Americans. But around 1968, with the help of President Lyndon Johnson's Great Society, the face of poverty turned black, and welfare became a problem of government dependence. In fact, economists Alberto Alesina, Edward Glaeser, and Bruce Sacerdote have shown that the primary reason we don't have a European-style welfare state is because the programs are seen to benefit black people. For them, "race is the single most important predictor of support for welfare."

Most white Americans today tend to see poverty in individual instead of systemic terms, having much to do with our national commitment to individualism. But African Americans know that whatever the system is, it is rigged in the favor of white people. It's not just about "initiative."

For some of us, we only have to talk to members of our family to get a sense of how things were, or still are, rigged. My great-grandmother Ruby Wilson worked as a domestic for white people in my hometown for almost thirty years. She never talked about that job or the people she worked for. No one told us, but we knew the subject was taboo. She didn't hate those people; she just understood them for who they were. When I came home from college angry about racism, she simply said,

"You better not dwell on that. That stuff will eat you up." Her pension plan amounted to the dimes she saved—dimes that bought the stove that cooked amazing pinto beans, and the refrigerator, or ice box as she called it, that held the best Kool-Aid in the world. Talking with her gave me a sense that some people had it better in life than others. Not because they had more individual initiative or were more disciplined. She worked tremendously hard. They were simply white.

None of this seems to matter in the broader public debate. African Americans who are struggling to find a job or keep a roof over their heads are often seen, especially by those on the right, as lazy or gaming the system (they buy steaks with food stamps!). If they are unsuccessful or poor, it is a reflection of bad character and bad choices, not a shortage of opportunities.

Even deadly encounters with the police indicate a failure of character. In response to the death of Michael Brown, Ben Stein, the actor and conservative commentator, had this to say:

> *The idea of calling this poor young man unarmed when he was 6'4"*
> *300 lbs full of muscles, apparently according to what I read in* The
> New York Times *on marijuana, to call him unarmed is like call-*
> *ing Sonny Liston unarmed or Cassius Clay unarmed. He wasn't*
> *unarmed. He was armed with his incredibly strong, scary self. . . .*
> *There was a time . . . when lynchings of African Americans were not*
> *that incredibly rare. Now the lynchings are of the police. It's just an*
> *outrage. Notice in both this case, just as in Trayvon Martin's case, it*
> *is the very large so-called victim attacking the policemen, who winds*
> *up dead. If they would not attack the police, if they would just talk*
> *to the policemen in a reasonable way no one would be dead.*

There is so much going on here that it is difficult to know where to begin. Stein magically transforms George Zimmerman, a wannabe neighborhood watchman, into a police officer. He claims Michael Brown was "armed" just by being "his incredibly strong, scary self"— like he is describing King Kong. Moreover, Brown's failure to submit to authority caused his death, not Darren Wilson, who pulled the trigger.

As if this isn't enough, Stein drops a history lesson in the middle of his rant. Once upon a time, the lynchings of black people "were not that incredibly rare." Now the police are the victims of lynchings. (A Fox News guest, Ron Hosko, went so far as to say, "Mr. Holder, it's time to cut Darren Wilson down from that tree.") We've put behind our troublesome racial past only to face reverse racism. Black people are no longer the victims of discrimination and racial violence. The police are. And, by implication because they are principally tasked to protect them, white people are.

It's easy to dismiss the views of Stein and others as those of a radical right-wing fringe. But Stein said out loud what poll data confirmed. Sixty-two percent of white St. Louis County residents believed that Wilson was justified in killing Brown. When asked whether the shooting raised important questions about race in this country, African Americans overwhelmingly said yes (about four to one). The majority of white respondents said that the issue was getting more attention than it deserved. Stein couched these racial attitudes within a broader story about the country. For him, we have put all of this behind us—except for a few racist lunatics. The problems black people face today, like the problem Michael Brown created for himself, are primarily of their own doing.

And that's just crazy, because most black people have known for some time that the problem with this country isn't *us*. It's *white* folk.

The value gap persists, in part, because of our national refusal to remember and our unwillingness to see what is right in front of our eyes. To declare ourselves a bastion of democratic life when black infant mortality is twice that of whites; when the level of inequality between the rich and the poor surpasses that of any other nation in the industrialized world; and when the United States has the highest documented rate of incarceration in the world—such a declaration is galling. Given this gap, the idea, one so powerfully expressed by Martin Luther King, that the nation must experience a fundamental change of the heart is not some sentimental, apolitical notion that ignores structural matters. It reflects, instead, that closing the value gap has both moral and political significance. We have to become better people by fundamentally transforming the conditions of our living together. This will require setting aside our comforting illusions.

When I say that the value gap is rooted, in part, in our national refusal to remember, I am not invoking some politically correct notion of history that simply includes previously excluded groups. How we collectively remember is bound up with questions of justice. Or, to put the point differently, what we choose to forget often reveals the limits of justice in our collective imaginations. Think about this in a personal way. Imagine that a family, one that prides itself on the strength of familial bonds, carries the burden of a terrible secret. Everyone knows, even as they act like they don't, that an adored relative has sexually abused a young niece repeatedly. Family gatherings go on as if nothing has happened or is happening. As time passes, stories are told about his sense of humor, his generosity in times of need, and his loving personality. With each recollection, the memory of his heinous actions falls into the shadows and the injustice of his treatment of his niece is ignored or forgotten—except by the victim herself. For her, stories of his kindness tell her, in effect, to shut her mouth.

When we *disremember* an event, an egregious moment in the past, we shape how we live in the present. I borrow the word from Toni Morrison. In her magisterial novel *Beloved*, she grapples with the difficulty of memories, haunting memories that come back to consume.

Disremembering enables the characters in the novel to ward off, temporarily, the pain of past events. Disremembering blots out horrible loss, but it also distorts who the characters take themselves to be. Something is lost. It is this sense of the word that strikes me as particularly useful for our current moment. Disremembering is active forgetting.

We forget particular moments for specific reasons. Speaking at an event sponsored by Iowans for Tax Relief in 2011, former U.S. Representative Michele Bachmann said, without any hint of irony, that the United States was founded on racial and ethnic diversity and that the founding fathers were responsible for abolishing slavery. Let's acknowledge for a moment that Bachmann has on a number of occasions revealed her scant knowledge of American history (she even declared John Quincy Adams one of the men who drafted the Constitution). If I were to criticize her simply for getting the facts wrong, you might accuse me of going after low-hanging fruit, but that's not what I'm interested in. What's important here isn't the gaffe itself but what its content reveals about how Bachmann disremembers the past. For her and her Tea Party supporters, America has *always* been good. Even when we were wrong, we were right. So in this misstatement of fact, the image of America as an ethnic melting pot, an Ellis Island image, is read back onto our national beginnings and the end of slavery is seen as part of our founding. The value gap gets completely lost in her insistence that America has been abolitionist since its beginning.

What we put in and leave out of our stories tells us something about who we are. The Fourth of July, Memorial Day, Presidents' Day, and Martin Luther King Day are public rituals that tell a particular story about our national journey. That story often involves accounts of heroic efforts or extraordinary events that make us feel good about ourselves and loyal to our country. The United States is not unique in this. All countries do it. But all too often, how we tell our story keeps us from seeing aspects of the past that may call into question the American Idea.

In 1834, during our national celebration of the Fourth of July, for example, African Americans who dared to join the activities were attacked, as their mere presence challenged the story of America. How could America be celebrated as a bastion of freedom when the very bodies of black folk suggested otherwise? We don't talk much about the Trail of Tears, the forced removal of Native Americans from their lands as a result of the Indian Removal Act of 1830, or about the evil of lynching (between 1887 and 1906, an African American was lynched in the South every four days). We may read about this stuff in a textbook, but we rarely question America's self-understanding as a beacon of freedom.

Even when we confront the more challenging aspects of our past, we do so to corroborate our goodness. When we see images of fire hoses turned on peaceful protesters in Birmingham, Alabama, in 1963 or watch the trauma of slavery in a film like *Twelve Years a Slave*, it is someone else's story. We stand in judgment of the past, but rarely in self-judgment.

Collective forgetting is crucial in determining the kind of story we tell ourselves. Ours is the chosen nation, the "shining city upon a hill," as Ronald Reagan called it. America *is* democracy. Anyone, no matter his humble beginnings, has a chance to make his dreams come true here. That's our story. To believe this, we have to forget and willfully ignore what is going on around us. Forget that for much of our history black people have had to wage a relentless war against white supremacy. Forget that now our class structure is so rigid that you probably have a better chance of winning the lottery than getting out of poverty if you are born poor. Forget all the bad stuff that cuts short the illusion that we are an example of democracy already achieved.

Our silence about the suffering throughout the country conspires with injustice. People who have suffered from past wrongdoings and present failings find it difficult, if not impossible, to call attention to their suffering when a precondition for American civic life is that only certain events can be recalled and must be recalled in certain ways. We have to talk about racism in a certain way. Dr. King is the model. We have to invoke love and nonviolence. Talk of white supremacy isn't allowed. We have to talk about poverty in a certain way. "Ladders of opportunity" are better than redistributive economic policies or what some call "class warfare." To ignore this is to risk being accused of trading in victim talk or, worse, to be declared "not one of us"—a traitor. The primary purpose of disremembering is to hide from view the value gap and to protect our national innocence: to keep the ugliness of our deeds at arm's length or buried deep in our national subconscious.

This is part of the sinister work of the value gap. We laud our democratic virtues to others and we represent ourselves to the world as a place of freedom and equality, all while our way of life makes possible choices that reproduce so much evil, and we don't see it happening—or, worse, we don't want to know about it. James Baldwin's words haunt: "People who shut their eyes to reality simply invite their own destruction, and anyone who insists on remaining in a state of innocence long after that innocence is dead turns himself into a monster." Are we a nation of monsters?

What is required, if America is to become the nation it hopes to be, is a wholesale transformation of our idea of who we are. This must involve confronting, without flinching, the nasty implication of the value gap. We must tell ourselves a different story, about how this belief has devastated the lives of so many Americans and how it has warped our idea of democracy. We can no longer forget. Such forgetting leaves in place the habits and illusions that make possible the value gap and sanctions our willful blindness to the devastation caused by the Great Black Depression.

We have to do better. And this will take much more than lofty appeals to the American Idea—the delusion that somehow, if we live up to our principles, all will be well once again in America. Illusions will not save us; they have to be smashed. We have to change fundamentally, and that will require uprooting the racial habits that are the lifeblood of the value gap.

CHAPTER THREE

RACIAL HABITS

When I was eight years old or so, we moved from one side of my small hometown in Mississippi to the other. It was a journey of contrasts. On the east side of Moss Point (named after the Spanish moss that hangs from magnolia trees) lived, for the most part, working-class and poor black folk. People worked hard either at the shipyard or at the paper mill. Homes were relatively modest and poverty was always in sight. On the west side lived mostly white folk. There were a few prominent black families there, too. Mostly executives or mid-level managers of some sort, teachers, or politicians. The difference between the landscapes of these two sides was obvious. The west side had sidewalks instead of dirt pathways and neighborhoods with two-story waterfront houses. This was June of 1976.

We moved into a sparsely integrated west-side community up on a hill called Briarwood Circle. My dad, the second black person hired at the post office in Pascagoula (the town next to Moss Point), tells the story of police slowly driving by, eyeing him through the car windows. He boldly dangled his house keys in the air and shouted, "Yes, I own it!" About a week later, the children of the neighbors in the back shot out the patio window with a pellet gun. My dad responded by shooting a twelve-gauge shotgun in the air as fair warning.

Most of the details of these early days escape me. I was too young. But I do remember one incident. It was the first time I was called a nigger.

On our first full day in the new neighborhood, I was playing Tonka trucks with the kid across the street. He had his truck. I had mine. We made engine noises, the kind when your lips vibrate. I can't remember his name. We played together only once. As we pushed dirt into a pile, readying it to load in the dump truck, I heard a loud yell from the boy's father: "Get over here. Stop playing with that nigger." I don't remember much after that. I think the boy looked at me. I looked at him. When I recall the moment, even today, I want to believe his eyes said he was sorry. I grabbed my truck and went inside.

It is ironic that racism first wounded me at the very moment my family experienced the fulfillment of the American dream—a big house on the "white side" of town. It was a reminder of the limits of dreaming in this country: for us, the ugliness of America was always just beneath the surface of our supposed racial progress. My father, although he wouldn't admit it, bore the wounds of that experience. He held a deep distrust of white people that bordered on hatred. That shouldn't be surprising, considering that he grew up in Jim Crow Mississippi, but white people often seem surprised when black people are angry. One can imagine my father's horror and rage when I told him what happened. He stared at me for a moment, as if his past were crowding in on him, and stormed outside.

All of this is a familiar account of how racism historically worked in this country—especially in a state like Mississippi: somebody hurls a racist insult, and that moment, in all of its ugliness, begins the lifelong work of fortifying the belief that such a view is a lie, that you're not a "nigger."

But we have to think about racism and the persistence of racial inequality in ways that go beyond the cruel act of someone's father calling an innocent child a nigger. Overtly racist acts like that are increasingly rare in this country; after all, it is decidedly out of fashion these days to be a racist. And these kinds of acts and actors, while terrible, no longer sustain racial inequality. Rather, inequality comes from the habits we exercise daily—habits that aren't revealed in racial slurs or blatant acts of discrimination, but in the choices we make and the lives we live, even when those choices and lives seem to have little to do with race.

Racial Habits

All Americans are shaped by biases, stereotypes, and the history of racism in this country that incline us to treat certain people in certain ways. We are shaped by our racial habits. And those habits in turn shape not only our lives and personal choices but the policies we create that reinforce the value gap.

Racial habits are the ways we live the belief that white people are valued more than others. They are the things we do, without thinking, that sustain the value gap. They range from the snap judgments we make about black people that rely on stereotypes to the ways we think about race that we get from living within our respective communities. Both shape how we account for the persistence of racial inequality today.

Everyone possesses racial habits, often without even realizing it. Habits, in general, predispose us to see our world in particular ways, and often we consider them helpful things. They save us time and effort, because we don't have to think about every small decision. You notice that your shoe is untied. You bend down and tie your shoe. It's as simple as that.

Well, maybe not so simple. Scientists have isolated neurological tissue in our brains, known as the basal ganglia, as the storehouse of our habits. Here our brains convert some of the stuff we do every day into automatic routine. This is called "chunking," and we rely on these "behavioral chunks" in our daily lives. For example, when I first learned how to ride a bicycle I found myself thinking about every detail. Balancing the bike. Holding on to the handlebars. Pedaling. Avoiding that damn mailbox. Now, even though I haven't ridden a bicycle in years, I could just get on one and the basal ganglia would do its work and the habit of riding of a bike would take over.

But habits aren't limited to personal acts like riding a bike. They are also social. They involve our interactions with and ideas about other people. In fact, when habits work successfully, they become a part of how we move about in our social lives, often residing in the background, unbeknownst to us.

Racial habits are a particular kind of social habit. We hold them because we have grown up in a country that values white people more than others. We learn this not by way of overt racism but through the details of daily life, like when we experience the differences in the quality of schools we attend, the different nature of our interactions with the police, the different ways we navigate where we work, our different neighborhoods, and the daily barrage of signals and cues about race that all Americans get through television and in news reports.

Not only do these habits shape how we interact with people of different racial backgrounds, they also guide how we think about and value groups collectively. And like many habits, they are formed when we are young. Take, for example, my family's move to the west side of Moss Point. I had already learned a lot about race and racial inequality, even though I was eight years old, before my new neighbor's father called me a nigger. White people were expected to live in one place and black people in another. Of course, there were exceptions, but the exceptions proved the rule.

And the differences between the two sides of town silently but powerfully communicated a lot about the racial order of things and the expectations I should have about my life. Our old neighborhood flooded every time we had a heavy rain, because of bad sewage pipes. My brother's all-black baseball team played on a field that wasn't as good as those across town. The houses weren't as big. The schools weren't as good. Everything about my environment taught me unspoken ideas about race.

We learn race in the places we live not as rules, but as habits—as a kind of general know-how that enables us to get about. We learn that there are places where *they* live and places where *we* shouldn't go. In fact, I had already been habituated to race at eight years old, because I knew we were moving not to a nicer part of town, but to the "white side" of town. Getting called a nigger, painful as it was, was just the icing on the cake.

Racial habits are formed by the outcomes we see in the world rather than by the complex processes that produced those outcomes. We see black and white sides of town and internalize certain assumptions about what that separation means, but rarely are those assumptions informed by the history of deliberate policies that created a dual housing market and residential segregation. We simply live where we live. We see double-digit black unemployment and infer things about black people from this statistic, but we rarely invoke the history of unfair labor practices, the exclusion of black people from labor unions, or the dual labor market that tracked certain folks to certain jobs. Responding based on habits formed without context, it's no surprise that so many white Americans today believe black people are lazy: that they don't want to work and are looking for a government handout.

These assumptions about black people and homeownership, about black folk and work, about crime, sex, education, health, and politics, are all rooted in an ugly racist history that we like to believe we've put behind us. After all, we dismantled legal segregation, and the majority of Americans say they are committed to racial equality. But the deed has already been done.

Just as I learned about race in my neighborhood when I was eight years old—not because I was instructed in the rules of the game but because the lessons were learned in the space I lived—we all now have racial habits that are the result of living for generations under the assumption that white people are more valued than others (and everything that follows from that). So, whenever we see or interact with someone of a different racial background we find ourselves traveling down furrowed pathways of behavior. Our racial habits are at work.

Racial habits express themselves in many different ways. On a basic level, many people simply respond to black faces with alarm or suspicion when none is warranted. We know the commonplace stories of women clutching their purses or crossing the street when they see black men. Store clerks around the country become extra diligent when particular kinds of people walk into their shops. Trayon Christian, a nineteen-year-old black college student shopping at Barney's in New York, was cuffed and taken into custody because the clerk didn't believe he could afford the $350 Ferragamo belt he had just bought.

Employers see names like LeKeisha or Lisa and make substantive decisions based on implicitly held assumptions about the names themselves, even though the résumés are exactly the same. Police officers patrol black neighborhoods in particular ways, and when they see a group of black male teenagers, certain assumptions about what they may be up to are triggered. Real estate agents decide to show prospective homeowners different neighborhoods and limit the options for some while expanding the options of others. In other words, a host of assumptions about who black people are and what they are capable of shape everything about how we live in this country.

Those assumptions have concrete effects. They result in fewer opportunities for African Americans to pursue their life dreams or to advance in their respective careers; they saturate our social world with stereotypes about laziness and criminality; they blind many Americans to the actual suffering in black communities. These assumptions, as evidenced in violent encounters with police, can also lead to premature death. Samuel DuBose, Sandra Bland, Tamir Rice, Michael Brown, Aiyana Stanley-Jones, Eric Garner, Tanisha Anderson, Trayvon Martin, and a host of others are clear examples of that fact.

But racial habits don't come out just in interactions between white people and black people. We're wrong when we think the problem of racial inequality rests simply with discrimination, whether by overt racists or people unconsciously enacting racial habits. This approach locates the problem elsewhere—with the bad people over there, safely securing most of us from the idea that our actions and snap judgments contribute, in any way, to racial inequality. Thinking in this way denies that the problem may be with the way we *all* live our lives, even in arenas that seem to have nothing to do with race. Something much more banal and pernicious is definitely at work.

Many social scientists, for example, have noted that high unemployment among African Americans may not solely be the result of racial discrimination. Black people may find themselves disadvantaged because they don't move around in the same social circles as white Americans. Seventy-five percent of white Americans report that their social networks are *entirely* white. Those networks refer them to potential employers and help them get jobs. Black networks don't seem to be as helpful; they aren't as robust or well connected. So help from family and friends may be the driving force of inequality in this country. White people extend a hand to those who are in their social circles, and they do so without any intention of disadvantaging others, but it still perpetuates white advantage.

When white Americans show favoritism in this way, they engage in what is called opportunity hoarding; that is, as members of a dominant group, they keep the good stuff (like education, jobs, capital) among themselves and create the conditions to continue keeping the good stuff. This habitual way of acting reproduces racial disadvantage.

Our racial habits hide this advantage. Americans of all colors insist that individual initiative and hard work are the keys to success. We believe in meritocracy, because we like to believe in the power of our abilities. But favoritism shows that this kind of robust individualism blinds us to the way social networks reproduce inequality: white individuals benefit from being part of white social groups. Nancy Ditomaso, Rochelle Parks-Yancy, and Corinne Post interviewed 246 randomly selected whites from New Jersey, Ohio, and Tennessee, and they said as much. As one white respondent said when asked whether he earned his place in life: "Did I earn it? Yeah, I worked for what I've got. Definitely. Nobody gave me nothing. Nothing." But this wasn't actually true. His father and his father's friends connected him with the construction union and helped him find better work. His social network gave him the opportunity, but talk of individual initiative and hard work rendered the advantage the network provided invisible to him.

With racial habits, white advantage shows up as the ordinary stuff of living. White people simply work hard and earn their opportunities. Black people, as one New Jersey respondent noted, are a "bunch of fucking lazy people. . . . They think the government owes them something. . . . You've got to go and get it. It's not handed to me. . . . They just . . . to me, they're lazy. I mean, point blank. They're looking for the easy way out." For him, racial inequality is not a problem of policy or politics; it is one of behavior. Interestingly, a friend gave this same person, who was applying for a job, a copy of the test *and* the answers. He said he wasn't so good in school.

It's not typically the case that Americans express their racial views as forcefully as this guy from New Jersey. We've reached a point in this country where we usually hide how we really think. It's a cultural norm to openly express a commitment to racial equality. So Americans have developed the habit of *masking*.

Americans consistently mask how they feel about racial matters. We habitually avoid the messiness of race issues. Most white Americans, for example, don't want to be seen as holding racist beliefs. Even though racial attitudes among whites have become progressively better, those attitudes don't necessarily square with their views about policies that seek to remedy racial inequality. In fact, 73 percent of whites believe blacks should not receive any kind of special favor to overcome inequality.

One respondent for the Whiteness Project, an interactive investigation of how white people experience their race, said as much: "I think it's hard to talk about race as a white person, because I feel like, maybe sometimes, black people are just looking for a reason to tell you why you're wrong or why you owe them something. If I was in a room full of white people I would not feel uncomfortable talking about race, but if there were other minorities in that room I might think a little bit different and I might be a little more careful opening my mouth to not offend anyone or to potentially get into an argument or heated debate." What this person describes happens all over this country as Americans gauge how they should behave in the presence of other racial groups. Another respondent put it bluntly: "You can't even talk about fried chicken or Kool-Aid without wondering if somebody is going to get offended. It's always like walking on eggshells, isn't it? I don't know. You don't know just where the line is."

African Americans, particularly those who have to work and live in predominantly white spaces, also engage in masking. We try to manage or mute any recognizable differences between others and ourselves. We may refuse to wear braids or dreadlocks. We might change how we talk in front of white people. I have even found myself laughing at an off-color joke in order to avoid appearing overly sensitive about racial matters (only to beat myself up afterward for doing so). In each instance, we put on a mask. We manage our own sense of difference by working hard to get others to think of us as normal or as like them. And in doing so we push the reality of racial inequality into the shadows, because we try to avoid the subject altogether. This happens as blacks and whites encounter each other—wherever we happen to meet.

Most of our habits are like this. They aren't instinctive. Instead, they are acquired in the context of a shared life with others—in our dealings with family and friends, in the particular places where we *experience* life. Habits reflect our general tendencies and dispositions, our sensitivities and predilections. These only matter in relation to other people. We also depend on them for a sense of continuity in our lives and a sense of control. Habits give the flood of our experiences some semblance of order in that they enable us to move about, with regard to some aspects of our lives, unreflectively. They become an intimate part of who we are, and once rooted, they take hold of us.

To see how racial habits hold sway we need look no further than our lack of national will to address the persistence of racial inequality. Americans have gotten used to double-digit unemployment in black communities. The staggering number of African Americans in prison or under some form of criminal supervision is not a cause for moral panic. The fact that hundreds of thousands of black children struggle every day to eat and attend failed schools doesn't raise a national alarm. This state of affairs reveals what researchers call the *racial empathy gap*.

In a study conducted at the University of Milano–Bicocca, researchers measured the biophysical responses of white participants to a video showing skin touched by a needle or an eraser. Ordinarily when we see someone in pain, it triggers a reaction in the same area of the brain where we experience our own pain. But white participants reacted differently to white people in pain than they did to black people. This was not a matter of disregarding the pain of black people but an assumption that the pain wasn't even felt by black people.

This isn't a matter of racial prejudice. It stems from the belief that African Americans have been made resilient by racism. So black people can endure more pain than others. This can help us understand the deafening silence about the suffering and pain caused by the Great Black Depression. Racial habits render it invisible.

So how do we start to change our racial habits? It's not easy. We enter a world not of our own making. People already have a sense of what is good and bad, what is appropriate and inappropriate. Tradition and history matter. Values, which go beyond our individual desires, matter. We learn this race stuff, and in some ways we have little choice. The young boy playing with me that first day in my new neighborhood learned something about his father and about me. He learned what was acceptable to someone he loved and what was not. He also learned, whether he understood it fully or not, that people like me were niggers. Later in life, I would like to believe he had a choice whether to live in accordance with those beliefs or consciously change them.

Habits are not fixed forever. If we are aware of their presence in our lives, we can change them. But we can't just look inside ourselves and solve the problem.

If habits are formed in our social world, then focusing only on what's happening inside our heads won't do the job. Only by changing the world we live in will we change the choices it prompts us to make. If we want to change our racial habits, we have to transform bad schools where the majority of black children learn; stop housing a disproportionate number of black people in prisons, jails, or halfway houses; and remake the places where we live that keep us ignorant of each other. We can't do it all at once. But our efforts might lead us to examine the practices and beliefs that give the value gap life.

Wendell Berry, the Kentucky-born writer, makes this point in his powerful book *The Hidden Wound*:

> *I am trying to establish the outlines of an understanding of myself in regard to what was fated to be the continuing crisis in my life, the crisis of racial awareness—the sense of being doomed by my history to be, if not always a racist, then a man always limited by* the inheritance of racism, *condemned to be always conscious of the necessity not to be a racist, to be always dealing deliberately with the reflexes of racism that are embedded in my mind as deeply at least as the language I speak. (Emphasis added.)*

In short, we are all shaped by racial habits in some way or another. They are as natural to America as apple pie and fireworks on the Fourth of July, and come to us as easily as the words we've learned since we were at our mother's knee.

In this sense, racial habits are our inheritance: they contain the history of white supremacy that has shaped and continues to shape this country. They are the millions of accumulated decisions that make racial inequality an inextricable part of what it means to be American. If we are to undo them (at least some of them), something dramatic must happen. And this is one reason the protests in Ferguson and Baltimore were so important. They forced us to confront our racial habits—to question how we police in this country and to see how black people are criminalized. In effect, they unsettled the racial sediment, and whether we were in the streets or not, agreed with the protests or not, we found ourselves, if just for a moment, examining the ugly reality of our racial habits.

In the end, we have to understand that we, as a nation, must be in *a continual crisis of racial awareness*—awareness of the ways we continue to consign large numbers of fellow Americans to the shadows for no other reason than because they are black.

Much of our national conversation and actions around race in this country deny the existence of racial habits. On the one hand, that denial reflects their effectiveness. They do their work unnoticed. On the other hand, Americans are often willfully blind to how those habits work—we don't want to see the racial inequalities all around us. Of course, most Americans acknowledge the wrongness of racist acts, and some give voice to the aspiration of a color-blind society. But neither view recognizes the racial habits that make possible our embrace of the ideas of equality and our comfort with persistent racial inequality.

How can we not see racial habits in action? It's largely because we don't have an effective method of dealing with race that engages our racial habits. Because racial habits are hidden in plain sight, most of us deal openly with race only when some ugliness bubbles up. A cop kills a twelve-year-old kid or a madman kills nine black people in a church. Protests erupt in a city because of it. We mistakenly think that the resolution of our race problems occurs in these moments, but it doesn't, largely because the way we deal with them as a society is more theater than substance. Like a classic tragedy, this theater serves a function, releasing pent-up energies caused by whatever racial incident sparked the conversation in the first place. Some politician or television personality announces that we need to have a serious conversation about race. They say it will be difficult. On television, the usual pundits, especially the black ones, show up to tell us what is really going on. And then they will go away. Nothing fundamentally changes.

Racial theater is somehow the stand-in for actually confronting the problem. It lets us move on feeling like we've done something without challenging the order of things. And we tell ourselves after watching the special or listening to the conversation that we are all better people for doing so—that we are, at least, a bit less racist. But our racial habits remain completely intact.

The most disturbing example of this inability to talk substantively about race is how President Obama handles the subject. He replies to claims that he ought to develop a specific policy agenda to help African Americans with a quick dismissal: "I'm not the president of black America. I am the president of the United States of America." His responses to African Americans reflect an overall attempt to avoid race matters or, minimally, to avoid being perceived as doling out favoritism to black people (although the deaths of African Americans at the hands of the police and the #BlackLivesMatter movement, in some ways, forced or freed him to talk more explicitly about race matters).

But for much of his presidency, Obama constantly contorted to avoid the racial land mines of American politics. The acrobatics affirm the troublesome idea that serious engagement with racial inequality in this country is anathema. The irony is glaring, isn't it? The first black president can't call attention to the racial habits that get in the way of genuine democracy, but his election can lead some to believe the illusion that we're post-racial.

When a jury of six women (five of whom were white) in Sanford, Florida, found George Zimmerman not guilty in the death of Trayvon Martin, President Obama initially responded to the verdict in this way:

> *The death of Trayvon Martin was a tragedy. Not just for his family, or for any one community, but for America. I know this case has elicited strong passions. And in the wake of the verdict, I know those passions may be running even higher. But we are a nation of laws, and a jury has spoken. I now ask every American to respect the call for calm reflection from two parents who lost their young son. And*

*as we do, we should ask ourselves if we're doing all we can to widen
the circle of compassion and understanding in our own communities. We should ask ourselves if we're doing all we can to stem the
tide of gun violence that claims too many lives across this country
on a daily basis. We should ask ourselves, as individuals and as a
society, how we can prevent future tragedies like this. As citizens,
that's a job for all of us. That's the way to honor Trayvon Martin.*

No mention of race. No call for a national policy initiative to address
racism and the criminal justice system. Just an appeal "to widen the
circle of compassion and understanding in our own communities." Our
racial habits went untouched.

A few days later, after a swell of protests around the country, President Obama spoke again. This time he explicitly identified with Trayvon Martin. Obama spoke in the White House briefing room:

*You know, when Trayvon Martin was first shot, I said that this
could have been my son. Another way of saying that is Trayvon
Martin could have been me 35 years ago. And when you think
about why, in the African American community at least, there's a
lot of pain around what happened here, I think it's important to
recognize that the African American community is looking at this
issue through a set of experiences and a history that—that doesn't
go away. There are very few African American men in this country
who haven't had the experience of being followed when they were
shopping in a department store. That includes me.*

*And there are very few African American men who haven't had
the experience of walking across the street and hearing the locks
click on the doors of cars. That happens to me, at least before I was
a senator. There are very few African Americans who haven't had
the experience of getting on an elevator and a woman clutching her*

purse nervously and holding her breath until she had a chance to get off. That happens often. And you know, I don't want to exaggerate this, but those sets of experiences inform how the African American community interprets what happened one night in Florida.

Here the president acknowledged racial profiling and sought to make the rage and disappointment throughout black America intelligible to white people. He then offered four concrete suggestions for a way forward for the nation: (1) professional training for police, in partnership with states and local governments, in racial bias; (2) examination of laws like "stand your ground"; (3) enlisting support through public-private partnerships, clergy, athletes, and entertainers to address the dismal condition of African American boys (what later became his My Brother's Keeper initiative); and (4) national soul-searching removed from the political arena that demands each of us examine our choices and actions to see whether we have worked hard to rid ourselves of the biases that perpetuate racism in this country.

These comments were just as ineffective as the first. Nothing about the social world that produces racial habits will change because of these recommendations. But liberal pundits, black and white, celebrated his words. Conservatives, meanwhile, accused him of stoking the fires of racial division. Others said that the comments were too personal, that he gave little indication of addressing racial habits at the policy level. In the end, as usual, nothing happened, and Trayvon Martin's parents are still grieving the loss of their son and the absence of justice.

President Obama's measured talk about race shows how racial habits work in this country. They work by keeping the reality of racial inequality hidden in plain sight. We can only talk about race as spectacle, not in terms of the daily choices we make that cut short the chances of so many black people. Something big has to happen for us to see the problem. It is not enough to indict cops or to convict George Zimmerman (although that would help). We have to get to the root of the problem—and that will require more than conversations that don't really advance the prospects of black folk, or even fully acknowledge America's problem with race.

Changing policies and addressing structural racism are the first steps toward undoing our racial habits. We also have to bring our ideas about black folk out into the open. We have to disrupt those accounts of black suffering that make us okay with the sad fact that some Americans—black Americans—are more likely to languish in poverty, to attend bad schools, to not have work, to lose their homes, to go to prison, or to bury their children killed at the hands of the police. We must remove our mask to call attention to white advantage. That may help us understand one another a bit better. It may bridge divides, disrupt assumptions and stereotypes that block empathy and get in the way of serious efforts to achieve our country. As it stands, we don't *really* talk frankly about race. And too many people are too damn scared to say so.

CHAPTER FOUR

WHITE FEAR

Richard Cohen, the *Washington Post* columnist, wrote a controversial op-ed after the verdict acquitting George Zimmerman in the death of Trayvon Martin was delivered. In Cohen's opinion, Zimmerman and white people, generally, have good reason to fear young black men: "Young black males commit a disproportionate amount of crime." That fact alone, Cohen argued, warrants suspicion of black men and justifies "stop and frisk" policies by police. The solution to such fear isn't a change in white people's attitudes, Cohen said. It requires changing black culture.

> [T]he least we can do is talk honestly about the problem. It does no one any good to merely cite the number of stop-and-frisks involving black males without citing the murder statistics as well. Citing the former and not the latter is an Orwellian exercise in political correctness. It not only censors half of the story but also suggests that racism is the sole reason for the policy. This mindlessness, like racism itself, is repugnant.

Cohen doesn't defend George Zimmerman. In fact, he explicitly says he "does not like what [he] did." But Cohen does believe Zimmerman was justified in fearing for his life, because young black men commit more crimes than others, and this makes it reasonable to fear *all* young black men.

Cohen's op-ed set off a firestorm. *Daily Kos* offered one of the more imaginative responses, listing data that contradicted the idea that white people should be afraid of young black men. The odds of a black person killing a white person are about 0.0000212. With those numbers, "[y]ou really have far more reason to be scared of say, getting on a ladder, than you do of getting murdered by the hoodie wearing teenager you see on the street. The fear is irrational." But that doesn't matter. Cohen believes this stuff, and he is not alone.

What matters for Cohen and for a large segment of white America was and is *white fear*. White fear is the general frame of mind that black people are dangerous, not only to white individuals because they are prone to criminal behavior, but to the overall well-being of our society.

White fear begins with logical feelings of unease about specific situations and spirals from there. It makes sense to be doubly vigilant when we drive in neighborhoods plagued by high crime rates. People, especially women, are mindful of the potential dangers of walking in a parking lot late at night. But that same vigilance can also lead us to perceive danger where it does not exist. The particulars of the situation don't really matter.

For instance: I was walking to my car one evening after a long day in the office when I saw the spouse of a colleague and raised my hand to say hello. But a peremptory glance let me know she was not interested. She seemed afraid. The fact that we've had dinner together and shared jokes, or that her partner writes about race, didn't seem to matter. I was black, and it was dusk.

She hurried along and I got in my car. It's Princeton. It's a patrolled campus parking lot. The black guy is wearing an expensive suit. Doesn't matter. The object of fear, in this instance, has only one identifiable quality: skin color. We see potential danger whenever we see *these* people.

White fear is a kind of political fear. Political fear (like the current fear of Muslims) reaches beyond fright or anxiety experienced by individuals. It's bigger than any one person. It is a deeply felt, collectively held fear shared by people who believe, together, that some harm threatens them and their way of life. That apprehension, based in how we generally live our lives and sometimes in individual experience, guides political choices and policy.

Here is the wildest and most devastating part. White fear isn't just limited to white people. As a political emotion, white fear is expressed across and within different groups—even among black people themselves. When I drive down Stuyvesant Avenue in Trenton, New Jersey, at night, I feel a deep concern about my own safety. Stuyvesant is not safe. In some quarters, it is known as "Little Iraq." Shootings, drug deals, and other illicit behavior happen on this street. But that "reasonable" concern is bound up with other assumptions about this particular street, and about the people who live there.

My particular sense of fear converges with broader assumptions and beliefs about Trenton, about cities (even small ones like Trenton), about African Americans, and especially about poor African Americans. In other words, I drive down Stuyvesant with an already developed sense of the danger of the space and of the people who inhabit it, because we learn from our society what is harmful and what is not.

This is how political fear works. It takes fears based in narrow concerns and gives them a more generalized feel: the specific fear that motivates *me* in this one instance ought to motivate me to be concerned about what matters *to us*, even if I am in no immediate danger. Intimate fears about encounters with individual black people become broader concerns about a general threat to the very fabric of our society. That threat, in turn, creates and nurtures our most intimate fears. It's a vicious circle.

S ince even before this country's founding, fears of black men have come from ideas and beliefs about who they are and about what they're capable of. Those ideas and beliefs circulated in newspapers and in popular culture, and eventually made their way into the first feature-length film in the United States, *The Birth of a Nation* (1915), which was based on the 1905 novel *The Clansman* by Thomas Dixon. They made black men subhuman. As the anti-lynching crusader and black feminist Ida B. Wells-Barnett put it: "[T]he world has accepted the story that the Negro is a monster, which the southern white man has painted him. And, today the Christian world feels, that while lynching is a crime . . . it cannot by word or deed, extend sympathy or help to *a race of outlaws* [emphasis added]." A race of outlaws or monsters is to be feared and policed, because they pose a threat not just to individuals but also to a cherished way of life.

Thus, white fear can be understood as something anticipatory, a fear just waiting to be expressed. It isn't based in any actual threat of harm. Instead, the *idea* of black violence or crime does all the work. The mere possibility of danger is enough to motivate us to act as if we are in immediate danger.

Such fears can produce cycles of *racial moral panics* in which black people are viewed as a threat to everything we hold dear. That perception shapes public sentiment and informs public policy debates as people call for directed efforts to address the crisis. For example, after emancipation, white fears about black male sexual desire for white women unleashed unimaginable terror and violence throughout the South. (Black women were always the object of sexual terrorism, during and after slavery, but never mind.) Black men dared to assert their equal standing in public life during this period, to assert their manhood. The idea of black manhood, expressed through full citizenship and evidenced in voting and economic success, produced fears of black men sleeping with white women.

Anxiety and panic ensued, so much so that in 1866 six former Confederate officers founded the Ku Klux Klan as a secret social club in Pulaski, Tennessee, to defend "the hallowed Southern way of life." By 1868, the Klan was terrorizing black men who tried to vote and, frequently, accusing those men of sexual liaisons with white women. In 1871, a congressional committee convened an investigation of the Klan's violence. It heard testimony across the South and soon discovered that black people who challenged white supremacy, especially those who stood accused of having slept with white women, were subject to unimaginable violence.

Henry Lowther, a black freedman from central Georgia, told the committee his story. One night about twenty disguised Klansmen came to his home. They accused him of taking "too great a stand against them in the Republican Party." He managed to get away safely. Lowther was later jailed and charged for conspiring to kill another black man, but denied a trial. This time he could not escape. Klansmen arrived in the middle of the night and took him to a swamp. "The moon was shining bright, and I could see them," he told the committee. They castrated him. The Klansmen not only condemned his work with the Republican Party, they accused him of "going to see a white lady."

Americans experienced several racial moral panics in the latter half of the twentieth century—all related to the fear of black criminality. As the nation confronted the grassroots social movements for black freedom, many Southern segregationists called for law and order in the face of the threat of the black criminal. Senator Strom Thurmond suggested that calls for integration would result in "a wave of terror, crime, and juvenile delinquency." At the 1964 Republican National Convention, presidential candidate Barry Goldwater was even more explicit:

The growing menace in our country tonight, to personal safety, to life, to limb and property, in homes, in churches, on the playgrounds,

and places of business, particularly in our great cities, is the mount-
ing concern, or should be, of every thoughtful citizen in the United
States. Security from domestic violence, no less than from foreign
aggression is the most elementary and fundamental purpose of any
government, and a government that cannot fulfill that purpose is
one that cannot long command the loyalty of its citizens.

For Goldwater and others, the mass demonstrations of the black freedom struggle—even Dr. King's nonviolent protests—amounted to
"bullies and marauders" running rampant in the streets.

Through the 1970s and 1980s, concerns over black lawlessness helped
morph the United States into the prison state it has become, as draconian
laws swelled prison populations throughout the country. Fears about
substance abuse and related violence were exploited by politicians and led
to a declaration of a war on drugs. The epidemic of crack cocaine, a drug
associated with poor black neighborhoods, drove that war into a heated
frenzy. Concerns over wild and lawless youth with their soundtrack of
rap music gripped the nation. The horror of the attack on the Central
Park jogger on April 19, 1989, only heightened the crisis as four black
youths and one Hispanic youth were accused and convicted of brutally
raping Trisha Meili after a night of "wilding." Politicians and scholars
alike fretted loudly over the new seemingly ultra-dangerous young black
men who threatened to rip through the very fabric of the nation.

The political scientist John J. Dilulio even coined the term *super-*
predator to call attention to this new breed of criminal, as dramatized
by the young men in the Central Park case. These were "kids that have
no respect for human life and no sense of the future," Dilulio said. They
were "fatherless, Godless, and jobless." For him, these were "stone-cold
predators." He even predicted that by 2000 "there would be a million
more people between the ages of 14 and 17 than there are now. . . .
Six percent of them will become high rate, repeat offenders—thirty

thousand more young muggers, killers, and thieves than we have now. Get ready."

The moral panic drove public policy as local, state, and federal governments began to imprison young black men and women at alarming rates. (Black women, for example, had the fastest-growing incarceration rates in the 1990s.) Black children weren't treated like children—they were increasingly tried in courts as adults.

Of course, Dilulio's findings were eventually proved incorrect. His data were wrong. There were no superpredators on the horizon. He even recanted his theory in 2001. "If I knew then what I know now, I would have shouted for preventions of crimes." The social costs and the lives ruined, however, cannot be undone. (The Central Park Five were exonerated in 2002.) White fear is the danger. Not black people.

Racial moral panics resulted in exaggerated outrage that increased policing of certain black communities, dulled even further capacities for empathy and compassion, and confirmed and deepened white fears. And we now have nearly one million African Americans incarcerated, which for many people, consciously or not, affirms the perceptions that started the cycle in the first place.

In 2014 the national media for a brief moment took up the horror of a supposed new game in American cities called "knockout." Videos on the Internet showed different groups of black men randomly "knocking out" unsuspecting strangers with one punch. The media was frenzied. News anchors were outraged. Lawmakers rushed to make the game a felony. Police announced more patrols. Panic gripped the public. You never know when or if it will happen to you. But whether or not the game had actually gone viral didn't ultimately matter. White fear was confirmed. As Philip Fisher writes in his important book *The Vehement Passions*:

This fear is general rather than individual, and its object is any possible other person, not one specific man facing me on the street at

night. It is also any possible time, not a specific moment, which after
all is an exceptional moment, one that will come to an end. This
fear never ends, never starts, is always present like gravity.

Here Fisher describes fear generally. But in the United States *white* fear
never ends either. It is always present, ready to be activated by the slight-
est encounter or gesture and ready to be used to short-circuit any serious
attempt to end racial inequality. And its gravitational force (the media)
pulls all Americans, no matter their color, into its orbit.

W hite fear more than almost anything else has driven the lightning-
rod incidents involving the unnecessary deaths of black people at
the hands of the police or armed whites. And yet we were supposed to
believe that the George Zimmerman trial had little, if anything, to do
with race. The system certainly tried to exclude it. Judge Debra Nelson
ruled in a pretrial hearing that the prosecution could use only the word
profiling—not *racial profiling*. Explicit reference to race was banished
from the proceedings. Juror B37 echoed this point. She insisted that
race did not play a role in what Zimmerman did. He'd simply judged
Martin's behavior in the context of a rash of burglaries in the neighborhood. As she put it, "I think [George] just profiled him because he was
the neighborhood watch, and he profiled anyone who came in acting
strange. I think it was just circumstances happened that he saw Trayvon
at the exact time that he thought he was suspicious."

But race was everywhere in this confrontation and in the trial. We
heard it in Martin's description of Zimmerman as "a creepy-ass cracker."
We saw it in Zimmerman's suspicion of Martin. We heard it in the testimony of Rachel Jeantel, the last person to talk with Martin before his
death, whose speech patterns and combative style on the witness stand
set off a firestorm in the press and on social media. Or when defense

attorney Mark O'Mara brought out a slab of concrete and claimed that it was a deadly weapon because Martin *could have* bashed Zimmerman's head into it. Trayvon was akin to the brute beast that Darren Wilson saw in Michael Brown. He was, in effect, the monster that our history had made him to be.

Zimmerman's "reasonable fear"—the threshold for his use of the "stand your ground" defense—was no ordinary response to a perceived threat. Trayvon Martin was a young black man, wearing a hoodie in a neighborhood in which Zimmerman thought he didn't belong. And in our culture, young black men dressed like Martin and in the "wrong" place are presumed dangerous. On Fox News, Geraldo Rivera went as far as to say that Martin was partly responsible for his own death, because he was wearing a hoodie. "When you see a kid walking down the street, particularly a dark-skinned kid like my son Cruz . . . what do they think? What's the identification, what's the association?" In those moments, a host of stereotypes about who black men are and what they are capable of are triggered. Rivera said as much. "It's those crime-scene surveillance tapes. Every time you see someone sticking up a 7-Eleven, the kid is wearing a hoodie. You have to recognize that this whole stylizing yourself as a gangster, you're gonna be a gangster wannabe? *Well, people are gonna perceive you as a menace.*" No matter what Trayvon Martin was doing (buying a bag of Skittles) or who he was (his father actually lived in the subdivision), he was invisible to Zimmerman. The stereotype of young black men as the menace described by Rivera obstructed Zimmerman's vision. The conditions for Martin's murder were set well before that fateful encounter. He was by definition a threat to someone's life.

Social-science research shows that people instantly categorize others on the basis of distinctions like race. Stereotypes are triggered when we encounter black people and, all too often, prejudice follows. That research also shows that in video simulations, people are more likely to shoot black men. In one study, white *and* black participants were more inclined to press "shoot" in the game when confronted by an unarmed black person than an unarmed white person. Police officers, even with their training, had similar results. These outcomes aren't inevitable. We can do something about them. But it requires that we acknowledge how racial stereotypes and bias affect how we see and respond to others. You just can't ignore racial habits, as Judge Nelson tried to do in the Zimmerman trial, and think that's the solution to such intractable problems.

In his freshman year at Brown University, my son, Langston, experienced what it means to be black and in the "wrong" place. His urban-studies professor assigned his group the task of observing one of the richest neighborhoods in Providence. Langston couldn't make the initial trip with his classmates to the neighborhood, so the next day, he went with his girlfriend to complete the assignment. They strolled into a park around 6:30 p.m. and sat down on a nearby bench. He pulled out his notebook and began writing down his observations. A bit later, a Providence police cruiser slowly drove by. The officers stared at him. The police car abruptly made a U-turn, turned on its blue lights, and drove onto the sidewalk, blocking any possible exit. An officer got out of the car. He shined a light into my son's face, then at his feet, and then near the shrubs and bushes. Never saying a word. Never acknowledging my son's existence. Langston finally asked, "Officer, can I help you?" The cop responded, "Who are you? Where are you from? And why are you here?" My son told him he was a Brown student and that he was completing a class assignment. The officer told him that the park closes at 9 p.m. Langston said, "I know, but it is only 7 p.m." The officer repeated, this time more forcefully, "The park *closes* at 9 p.m." At this point, his partner came around the car with his hand on his gun or Taser. My son put his hands up and said, "We don't want any trouble. We're leaving now."

As he told me the story on the phone later, I fumed. I had just received a call, not an hour earlier, informing me that I had been elected the next president of the American Academy of Religion, the largest professional organization of religion scholars in the world. That didn't matter. My status as a Princeton professor didn't matter. I knew that. I teach about this stuff. But this wasn't an intellectual argument or an example in a book. My only child was telling me that the police, one of them with his hand on a weapon, told him that his body was in the wrong place. He'd had reason to fear for his life. They could've killed him.

We talked. His emotions ranged from shock to anger. I told him, "Now imagine if you lived in a different place how often you would have to experience that."

Embargoing talk of race won't help us get at what motivated the officers to harass my child, or help us understand why Zimmerman decided to do what he did to Trayvon Martin, or help us as a nation get at the racial habits that drive our most intimate and generalized fears about black people. It certainly won't help us understand what it means when we discover police officers in North Miami using mug shots of African American men for target practice. Nor will embargoing race help us fathom how trained police could drive up on a twelve-year-old boy and, within two seconds, mistake him for a twenty-year-old man, reasonably fear for their lives, shoot him, and refuse to administer first aid. White fear blinds us to the humanity of the people right in front of us. It makes it easier to devalue them, to see them as a threat, to dispose of them without any discomfort or conscience.

White people aren't fearful of black people simply because they're white. That fear has a history. It has shadowed American life ever since we reconciled our commitment to democratic principles with the institution of slavery. That reconciliation required, among other things, white people to believe that their lives mattered more than others—that the benefits and burdens of democracy did not extend to black people. They were slaves or, at best, interlopers in this grand experiment in democracy.

Americans believe in democracy, *and* we are committed to white supremacy. Obviously, it is wrong to hold both views. White fear can rear its ugly head as a kind of moral anxiety when we recognize just how wrong this is, and consistently do nothing about it. Looked at like this, white fear is the belief that black people are dangerous; the danger, though, stems from the fear of black revenge or of God's punishment for our national sins around race.

This kind of fear—the fear, as Malcolm X said, "of the chickens coming home to roost"—is as old as America itself. In 1785, Thomas Jefferson wrote in *Notes on the State of Virginia*:

> *Indeed I tremble for my country when I reflect that God is just: that his justice cannot sleep for ever: that considering numbers, nature, and natural means only, a revolution of the wheel of fortune, an exchange of situation, is among possible events: that it may become probable by supernatural interference! The Almighty has no attribute which can take side with us in such a contest.*

Jefferson was obviously concerned with divine retribution. He feared the moral implications of holding another human being in bondage.

For Jefferson, this sense of fear was a consequence of racial habits learned in the context of living with slavery. Customs and manners were indelibly shaped by the transactions that slavery demanded. As Jefferson put it, "The whole commerce between master and slave is a perpetual exercise in the most boisterous passion." Slaves had to know their place or risk violent punishment. Masters had to exercise their power. Those caught in slavery's vise grips could see themselves and others only in particular ways: as those who owned people and as those who were owned. Slavery affected and deformed the character of slaveholders by creating habits of mind that distorted their moral sense. These habits were passed along to children. Jefferson wrote: "The parent storms, the child looks on, catches the lineaments of wrath, puts on the same airs in the circle of smaller slaves, gives a loose to his worse of passions, and thus nursed, educated, and daily exercised in tyranny, cannot but be stamped by it with odious peculiarities."

For Jefferson, white fear takes root here: in the habits formed as we live lives shaped by the ideas and practices of white supremacy and in the anticipation of the possible consequences that may follow from what we are doing to other people. Those habits carry with them, then, a kind of fear and trembling that someday, at some point, all of us, like sinners condemned to hell, will be held to account.

Jefferson is not alone. Abraham Lincoln echoed this haunting sense some eighty years later. In his second inaugural address, amid the carnage of the Civil War, Lincoln said:

Fondly do we hope, fervently do we pray, that this mighty scourge of war may speedily pass away. Yet, if God wills that it continue until all the wealth piled by the bondsman's two hundred and fifty years of unrequited toil shall be sunk, and until every drop of blood drawn with the lash shall be paid by another drawn with the sword, as was said three thousand years ago, so still it must be said "the judgments of the Lord are true and righteous altogether."

Lincoln characterized the war as, perhaps, God's punishment for the sin of slavery. Even in this most sacred of moments in American history, white fear as divine retribution haunted the nation.

And not just a reckoning from the heavens. Alongside the moral judgment has always been the fear that black people will exact their own vengeance—and that they'll be right to do so. Jefferson was concerned with the moral wrongness of bondage, but he also worried about black slave insurrection in the United States—a kind of deep and pervasive fear and paranoia about possible revenge.

The Haitian revolution confirmed those fears. In 1804, some nineteen years after Jefferson's expression of fear and trembling, Toussaint Louverture and Dessaline defeated Napoleon's armies, and Haiti became the first black nation in the new world. Napoleon's defeat sent shock waves throughout the slaveholding Americas. People feared that those forced to toil in the fields would inevitably turn their rage against their masters and that, given the moral abomination of slavery, God would take the side of the slaves. Slave rebellion would be divinely sanctioned.

In the first half of the nineteenth century, slave rebellions like those planned by Gabriel Prosser, Denmark Vesey, and Nat Turner scared the hell out of white slave owners. And the idea of weaponized black folk, talking about violence or self-defense, or calling for rebellion or revolution, has continued to scare the hell out of white folk. In the 1960s and 1970s, the Black Panther Party frightened white America. Young black men and women, with leather jackets and berets, carried guns and challenged state power. They called cops pigs and dared to speak openly of revolution. No wonder J. Edgar Hoover thought of them as "the most dangerous threat to national security" in America. The Panthers capitalized on white fear; they understood it and brought the anxieties of the country to a fever pitch. They wanted to make sure the status quo was uncomfortable.

But neither fear of divine retribution nor of black revenge was sufficient motivation to treat black people justly or to reimagine American democracy apart from white supremacy. Jefferson talked and wrote eloquently about democracy and the moral cost of bondage and, with rational efficiency, managed his slaves at Monticello. Lincoln denounced slavery, signed the Emancipation Proclamation, and considered the reasonableness of emigration/colonization schemes to rid the country of its black problem. For both, the presence of black people threatened the moral standing of the country and the moral character of its most valued asset—white Americans. White fear has never motivated people to look for solutions that would involve ameliorating the deep conditions that produced the fear in the first place. Instead, the response has been to eliminate the fear by eliminating black people. Either we needed to get rid of black folk physically or just make the whole damn country color-blind.

Such color-blindness would be rich in irony given another of white fear's many facets: the fear that genuine racial equality requires the end of white America. That would be the ultimate revenge—the disappearance of white folk altogether. Some believe that black freedom— economic, political, and otherwise—threatens the freedom of white people. The conservative *New York Times* columnist Ross Douthat wrote that many white people believe the nation is hell-bent on handing over the country to underrepresented groups; that all pathways to success for hardworking white people have been shut down. "This breeds paranoia, among elite and non-elites alike," Douthat noted. "Among the white working class, increasingly the most reliable Republican constituency, alienation from the American meritocracy fuels the kind of racial conspiracy theories that [Glenn] Beck and others have exploited."

Douthat isn't making this stuff up. Sixty percent of working-class white Americans believe that discrimination against whites is a bigger problem than discrimination against blacks. One respondent in the Whiteness Project put it this way: "It's my honest opinion that today it's the white race is the one that's discriminated against. . . . I have taken exams to get into the skills trades . . . and scored well on the exam, but didn't get picked for the apprenticeship programs, because minorities had to fill 'em, because of quota status. . . . I felt cheated and it wasn't fair." For him, racial equality amounts to taking opportunities from honest white Americans and giving them to people who haven't earned them—an un-American notion to its core. It is a zero-sum game.

A sign on an overpass on Interstate 640 in Knoxville, Tennessee, captures the underlying sentiment. Two vinyl banners about 30 inches tall and 123 feet long, stretching across the Norfolk Southern Bridge covering the width of the interstate, declared ANTI-RACISM IS A CODE WORD FOR ANTI-WHITE. For the people who put up the sign, true racial equality means one thing: a wholesale attack on white people and a deep-seated fear about what that might mean.

W hite fear is clearly dangerous to black people as individuals, and that fear affects how black people behave politically and how we respond more generally to racial inequality. The *fear of white fear* distorts black political behavior. We have to constantly censor our rage. I can't be "the angry black man." I can't call Bill O'Reilly a dumbass (at least not in public or on television). No matter the horror of the moment, our anger must be overcome and expressed reasonably out of concern of triggering white fear or making white folk uncomfortable under the weight of racial accusation. That's why black protesters must constantly allay national fears, no matter the context, by proclaiming their commitment to nonviolence. It's a litmus test to make sure you're one of "the good ones." Constantly policing what we say and how we feel, many African Americans often don the mask in public debate as our spirits wage war against the rage that threatens to consume us. We have to confront, every time we open our mouths, the possible consequences of making white people afraid. It can be exhausting.

One can see this in the political calculations of President Obama. His campaign speech on race in Philadelphia, considered one of the most important political speeches in recent memory, offers a great example of how a fear of white fear can work. Obama tried to account for the anger of the Reverend Jeremiah Wright by explaining that he was among those who grew up in a country that regularly defeated the dreams of African Americans. Wright's anger, then, was understandable, but its expression was unproductive. Obama then immediately juxtaposed Wright's anger with the anger of segments of white America. As he put it,

> [A] similar anger exists within segments of the white community. Most working- and middle-class white Americans don't feel that they have been particularly privileged by their race. . . . They've worked hard all their lives, many times only to see their jobs shipped overseas or their pensions dumped after a lifetime of labor. They are anxious about their futures. . . . Opportunity comes to be seen as a zero-sum game, in which your dreams come at my expense. So when they are told to bus their children to school across town; when they hear that an African American is getting an advantage in landing a good job or a spot in a good college . . . resentment builds over time. Like the anger within the black community, these resentments aren't always expressed in polite company.

Obama's approach gave the expression of anger in both instances the same moral weight. Such a move obscures the power of racial habits in determining the life outcomes of Americans. It makes it seem that black rage in the face of debilitating inequality is the same as white anger over the loss of white privilege. But this just deepens racial habits, as white Americans are led to believe that their anger toward black people is justified. It also gives license to those who routinely dismiss African American grievances as the cries of perennial victims.

In his address celebrating the fiftieth anniversary of the March on Washington—a sacred moment in African American history—Obama told a particular story of black struggle. That story involved a troubling account of the role of black anger. He said,

> *If we're honest with ourselves, we'll admit that during the course of 50 years, there were times when some of us, claiming to push for change, lost our way. The anguish of assassinations set off self-defeating riots.*
>
> *Legitimate grievances against police brutality tipped into excuse-making for criminal behavior. Racial politics could cut both ways as the transformative message of unity and brotherhood was drowned out by the language of recrimination. And what had once been a call for equality of opportunity, the chance for all Americans to work hard and get ahead, was too often framed as a mere desire for government support, as if we had no agency in our own liberation, as if poverty was an excuse for not raising your child and the bigotry of others was reason to give up on yourself. All of that history is how progress stalled. That's how hope was diverted. It's how our country remained divided.*

Nothing about this formulation rings historically true. The language of recrimination, I suppose, stands as a description of the rhetoric of the Black Power movement. But the other stuff is just the nasty rhetoric of the Reagan era that has sadly become familiar. Obama invokes the idea of black criminality, of black people looking for government handouts instead of working hard, of black parents failing to raise their children properly, and of false cries of racism as the excuse for troubles that are of our own making. This is the refrain of the neoconservatives who worked tirelessly in the 1980s and 1990s to undo the gains of the black freedom struggle.

President Obama trades in this kind of talk without any shame. His words stand as the flip side of the racial dog whistle. It's not that he seeks to trigger the racism of whites with coded language, as Republicans do with their talk of entitlements. Instead, with these words, Obama assuages, or so he hopes, the fears of white America. He confirms, at least for those who are listening, that he isn't some Manchurian candidate for black revenge.

White fear requires that we make white people feel comfortable about race. Black people have to be the "Uncle Remus" of American national politics: nonthreatening, loyal, and generally happy. If we are angry, we have to express that anger in a way that white people find politically acceptable. We have to march, vote for some Democratic candidate, or watch a gaggle of civil rights leaders hold a press conference and invoke the legacy of Dr. King—the King of 1963, mind you. It also entails translating the specific concerns of black communities into something more universal. The issue can't be all about black people. We have "to lift all boats." All of this happens because of one unmistakable fact: if we talk directly about black suffering in this country we risk alienating large segments of white America, jump-starting their fears. Without a hint of irony, this approach to race matters acknowledges the long-standing and dangerous racial habits lurking beneath our politics. And Barack Obama's election did little, if anything, to uproot them. In fact, he conceded to their terms.

Like most African Americans, President Obama worries that honest and direct conversations about race might produce feelings of guilt or a sense of accusation. But here I think Malcolm X got it right: "Stop sweet talking them. Tell them how you really feel. Tell them what kind of hell you've been catching. And let him know that if he's not ready to clean up his house—if he's not ready to clean up his house, he shouldn't have a house. It should catch on fire and burn down." In other words, we should remind America that chickens do, in fact, come home to roost.

CHAPTER FIVE

RESTLESS SLEEP AFTER KING'S DREAM

Malcolm X's insistence on "frank and fearless speech" may be just the remedy to how we dance around the subject of race in this country. Not that we should set white people's houses on fire (funny how calls to burn down the country don't make white Americans feel any better), but that we embrace his claim that only by telling the nation exactly "what kind of hell we've been catching" will we achieve true racial justice.

That's hard to do when the model for talking about racial justice in this country is a sanitized, cherry-picked version of Dr. Martin Luther King Jr. Every year when we celebrate his holiday, every Black History Month when we recognize his accomplishments, every time we dare take up the thorny issues of racial inequality, people invoke Dr. King, his commitment to nonviolence, and his dream as the best example of black struggle. One day after returning home from his fifth-grade Black History Month program, my son said, "Daddy, it's like Dr. King is the only person in black history."

Sometimes it feels that way. But it is always a particular version of Dr. King—the King of the March on Washington who dreamed, not the radical King who marched with garbage workers or understood the connection among the evils of poverty, racism, and militarism or called attention to the fact of "two Americas." This whitewashed King often gets in the way of frank and fearless discussions of black suffering, because his words, in the hands of far too many, are used to hide racial habits and sustain the value gap.

On September 20, 1966, in a small town in Mississippi, Dr. King would not get out of bed. Andrew Young, his closest adviser, tried everything. He used all the techniques they had learned over the course of the movement when any one of them faced debilitating exhaustion. Nothing worked. This was not exhaustion. King had fallen into a deep depression.

Barely removed from the euphoria of the 1963 March on Washington and his historic "I Have a Dream" speech, and the legislative triumphs of the Civil Rights Act of 1964 and the Voting Rights Act of 1965, Dr. King now confronted the uncertainty of his moral vision for the country. White America was not ready for racial equality. The violence against peaceful demonstrators marching for open and fair housing in Cicero, Illinois, a racist white suburb outside of Chicago, had made plain (though King knew this already) that racism was not a unique disease of the South. The hatred was clear, and it was American.

Dr. King and movement veterans faced a rising tide of white resentment based on the fear that true justice for black people meant robbing white Americans of something. Throughout the country, in statehouses and within the Beltway of Washington, D.C., some white Americans voiced their deep anxieties about the "lawlessness" of black political demonstrations. Ronald Reagan's gubernatorial campaign ran ads with footage of riots, a narrator ominously warning, "Every day the jungle draws a little closer." The series of legal victories that had climaxed with the Voting Rights Act of 1965 came to a grinding halt as white politicians pushed back against further legislation. The Civil Rights Act of 1966, which included, among other things, mandates for diversified juries, a commitment to "open and fair housing," and protection of civil rights workers, died in the Senate on September 19, the day before King took to his bed. The votes to end a southern filibuster could not be found.

King stood at the crossroads of a massive realignment of sentiment and strategy. The "Great White Switch," the change in partisan voting patterns among southern whites from the Democratic to the Republican Party, was under way, and the 1966 midterm elections saw Republicans make significant gains. President Johnson later famously lamented, "I don't think I lost that election. I think the Negroes lost it." Ronald Reagan won the governor's seat in California. In response to a question about his landslide victory and white resentment, Reagan simply said: "The people seem to have shown that maybe we have moved too fast." In this perverted sense, black people were the reason white people were racist. Their demands to be free and bitter denunciation of white supremacy made white people angry, reactionary, and more racist than ever. No wonder young black people called for black power.

King confronted the cries for black power emanating from the June 16, 1966, March Against Fear in Greenwood, Mississippi. Stokely Carmichael boldly declared at the march, "This is the twenty-seventh time I have been arrested—and I ain't going to jail no more! The only way we gonna stop them white men from whuppin' us is to take over. We been saying freedom for six years and ain't got nothing. What we gonna start saying now is black power!" Many young African Americans had grown impatient with King's calls for nonviolent, direct action and his invocations of love in the face of white violence. Love presumed that white America had a moral conscience. Many doubted that. Power or the lack of power was at the center of black misery in this country, they maintained. What black folk needed was real political power to secure and protect their interests, not an idea of love dependent on the transformation of white people's hearts.

The media frenzy around Black Power and the justified impatience of African Americans challenged King's insistence on the effectiveness of nonviolent protests and the relevance of love in the face of hatred and white retrenchment. He also struggled to come to terms with his organization's failure in Chicago. King would describe the racism in Cicero as the most "hostile and hateful" demonstration of white bigotry he ever faced. The shock of the Birmingham and Selma movements seemed like the distant past as white Americans tired of seeing how brutal white folk could be and as they calculated the real costs, for them, of racial equality.

King's bout of depression hit in the midst of the Southern Christian Leadership Conference's efforts to desegregate schools in Grenada County, Mississippi. There he saw, once again, the capacity for evil in those committed to white supremacy. As 150 black students entered John Rundle High School and Lizzie Horn Elementary, an angry mob gathered outside. White students were dismissed at midday. A half hour later, black students walked out of the school and found themselves surrounded. The mob attacked the children with fists, feet, pipes, and tree limbs. Grown men descended upon twelve-year-old Richard Sigh and broke his leg with pipes while others, laughing, pummeled a pig-tailed girl.

Perhaps Dr. King, like Baby Suggs in Toni Morrison's novel *Beloved*, had finally succumbed to marrow weariness: the ugliness of white folks, the folks who Baby Suggs knew could come into her yard anytime they wanted, made King beyond tired, a kind of spiritual fatigue that cut through the bone. Maybe he no longer could hold himself together. Marrow weariness always threatens to overwhelm hope: it involves the nastiness of life breaking through your defenses, leaving you with a sense of helplessness and a feeling of being terribly alone.

Desperate and panicked, Andrew Young asked Joan Baez, the American folksinger and activist, who had arrived in Grenada that weekend, to visit King and to sing for him. She sang, a cappella, "Pilgrim of Sorrow." Dr. King flashed a faint smile and began to stir. Baez had touched something.

> *Oh soon I shall reach the bright glory*
> *Where mortals no more do complain*
> *The ship that will take me is coming*
> *The captain is calling my name*

In her soul-stirring soprano, Baez sang a blessed assurance to Dr. King as he lay quietly in bed. "I think of the kind words of Jesus. Poor pilgrim I am always nigh." That faith lifted him up once again. So much so that he, with Baez, later that day escorted two young black girls to Lizzie Horn Elementary School. But King knew times were changing. He seemed alone in his belief that the moral stance of the movement offered a pathway for the nation's salvation, and the viciousness of white hatred didn't help matters much. Perhaps the last stanza gave him some hope and peace: "I've heard of a city called heaven. I've started to make it my home."

Two years later he would lie dead on the balcony of the Lorraine Motel with the right bottom quarter of his face blown off.

In the short time between his bout with depression in Grenada and his murder in Memphis, Dr. King came to understand the depths of American racism. He had underestimated how deeply rooted white supremacy was in the habits of American life. How the transformation of the heart he had so eloquently preached about since the 1955 Montgomery bus boycott required a fundamental change in the practices and structures of the country—change that could not depend solely on the moral conscience of white people, no matter black people's willingness to sacrifice and suffer, because of their investment in white supremacy.

In fact, in August of 1967, King stated plainly, "The vast majority of white Americans are racists, either consciously or unconsciously."

The commitment to the idea that white people were superior to others distorted the principles of democracy and disfigured the moral character of those who believed it. King had seen it up close in the contorted faces of sheriffs in small southern towns and in the ferocity of young white toughs in Cicero. He remained committed throughout to the moral power of his call to the nation—he never stopped being a preacher—but he now understood that something far greater was required if America was to be redeemed.

Just two months after struggling to get out of bed in Grenada, he offered this analysis at an SCLC retreat in St. Helens, South Carolina: "The fact is that the ultimate logic of racism is genocide. If you say that I am not good enough to live next door to you . . . because of the color of my skin or my ethnic origins, then you are saying in substance that I do not deserve to exist." Uprooting racial habits along with his criticisms of capitalism and the war in Vietnam set the terms of his challenge to the staff of SCLC and to the nation. This is the radical King, the mature King.

Few, however, were listening. In 1967, for the first time in a decade, Dr. King was not listed on the Gallup Poll of the ten most-admired Americans. Young African Americans in ghettos throughout America questioned his relevance to the freedom struggle. They now looked to the words of Malcolm X and the example of the Black Panther Party. In four short years, King had fallen from the heights of the Lincoln Memorial, where he delivered a speech that would become a crucial document in the history of our country, to the lowly status of a lone voice in the wilderness: a voice marginalized by many white liberals, castigated by white conservatives, and dismissed by some black militants.

This period of King's career remains in the shadows of our contemporary celebration of his legacy. It is as if he always represented the best of American ideals—that a bust of his likeness was destined, from the beginning, to be in the Oval Office. The fact that King was once viewed as an enemy of the state, a troublemaker who dared to challenge southern segregation, or that he spent much of his last years dismissed and demonized because of his opposition to the Vietnam War and his fearless criticism of the triple evils of racism, capitalism, and militarism—all this complex history of the man and of the nation gets buried under the fragment of his body of work that corroborates the illusion of color-blindness.

For many Americans of whatever color, Dr. King has become a four-word sentence: "I have a dream." And that sentence is often tied to his aspirational claim: that his "four little children will one day live in a nation where they will not be judged by the color of their skin but by the content of their character." Ironies abound. The man who sacrificed his life to dislodge the precious ideals of democracy from the stranglehold of white supremacy has now become the lead actor in the last staging of the tragedy of race in this country.

Dr. King's dream should not be read as a desire for color-blindness. In the context of the entire speech, his hope for his children stands as a criticism of our racial habits. As he stated in the "I Have a Dream" speech: "We can never be satisfied as long as our children are stripped of their selfhood and robbed of their dignity by signs stating FOR WHITES ONLY."

But this criticism of white supremacy is eclipsed in our collective memory by the parts of his legacy that are more useful to those who wish to reinforce the value gap. King has been and continues to be put to perverse political uses. Various interests on the right and left deploy his legacy and words to justify dismantling race-specific policies or to authenticate their own limited liberal vision. In order to use him in our current political theater, King has to be *disremembered*.

A s I suggested a few chapters ago, disremembering involves *active* forgetting. Societies disremember all the time; in fact, it seems to be an intimate part of collective memory itself. Societies bury the historic wrongs that lie beneath their feet and tend to remember their heroes and heroines minus the darker sides of their characters. But disremembering historic wrongs leaves vulnerable those among us who are the inheritors of historic wounds, who still bear the scars of past collective deeds (for example, those who once possessed these lands, the descendants of ex-slaves, of forced migrant laborers, and a host of others). Public disremembering, in these instances, amounts to a special offer: if we all join in the collective forgetting, no matter the vested interests that call us to forget in the first place, we make possible a shared sense of destiny. But that sense of shared destiny almost always comes at too high of a cost: our silence and invisibility.

This is what President Woodrow Wilson reached for on July 4, 1913, at a gathering of Union and Confederate veterans to celebrate the fiftieth anniversary of the Battle of Gettysburg. Assembled about him were white men wearing Union and Confederate uniforms. One even held a small Confederate flag. Wilson, the first southern president since the Civil War, declared the "quarrel forgotten."

> *We have found one another again as brothers and comrades in arms, enemies no longer, generous friends rather, our battles long past, the quarrel forgotten—except that we shall not forget the splendid valor, the manly devotion of the men arrayed against one another, now grasping hands and smiling into each other's eyes. How complete the union has become and how dear to all of us, how unquestioned, how benign and majestic, as state after state has been added to this, our great family of free men!*

For Wilson, the future opens up precisely because the past has been actively forgotten. No recall of slavery. No mention of the costs of reconciliation between the North and South for those once enslaved. As one historian put it, "The 1913 'Peace Jubilee' . . . was a Jim Crow reunion, and white supremacy might be said to have been the silent, invisible master of ceremonies." The terror of lynching and the brutality of legal segregation shadowed Wilson's soaring rhetoric. His was a ritual act of disremembrance: a public performance of recalling and *not* recalling aimed at setting the future free from the sins of the past.

In so many ways, our yearly celebration of Dr. King is a ritual act of disremembrance. It is a memorialization of a particular understanding of him (without his criticisms of white supremacy, poverty, and empire) designed to fortify the illusion of color-blindness in a country with dramatic racial inequality. Even the website of the King Center makes use of this view of Dr. King: "The King Holiday honors the life and contributions of America's greatest champion of racial justice and equality, the leader who not only dreamed of a color-blind society, but who also led a movement that achieved historic reforms to help make it a reality." Here color-blindness demands that we forget the unfinished business of the past in the promise that such forgetting will make for us a more just society. We are to remember Dr. King, and the movement he represented, as a sentimentalized proponent of nonviolence and total love. That's all. The other stuff gets tossed in the trash bin, discarded bits of willfully forgotten history.

RONALD REAGAN'S KING

On a picturesque autumn day in the White House Rose Garden, President Ronald Reagan signed the Martin Luther King Day bill into law. As if engaged in a ritual act of penance, each year after his death until 1983, Congress had entertained legislation seeking to honor Dr. King with a federal holiday. Each year the bill had failed. Some congressmen argued that it was too expensive to create a new federal holiday. Others, like Senator Jesse Helms, just outright hated the idea of celebrating someone he believed was a communist agitator.

But, on this Wednesday in 1983, President Reagan invoked the words of John Greenleaf Whittier, one of the Fireside Poets, a Quaker and an ardent abolitionist. He quoted a line from Whittier's 1880 poem "The Lost Occasion": "Each crisis brings its words and deed." For Reagan, at least on this occasion, King's sacrifice "stirred our nation to the very depths of its soul."

It was a wonderful touch for the man who announced his candidacy for the White House in notorious Neshoba County, Mississippi, the place where the civil rights workers James Chaney, Michael Schwerner, and Andrew Goodman were murdered. "I believe in states' rights," Reagan had told the crowd then, just three years before.

I believe in people doing as much as they can for themselves at the community level and at the private level. And I believe that we've distorted the balance of government today by giving powers that were never intended in the Constitution to that federal establishment.

Reagan's invocation of states' rights in the bowels of the South called up a complex racial history where big government was aligned with demands for racial equality that threatened "the southern way of life," and implicitly harkened back to the Dixiecrat Revolt of 1948.

In the Rose Garden, however, Reagan did not hold forth on the perils of big government. Instead, he told a brief story of the civil rights movement, a story that confirmed for him the "sense that true justice must be color-blind, and that among white and black Americans, as [King] put it, their destiny is tied up with our destiny, and their freedom is inextricably bound to our freedom; we cannot walk alone." It was a familiar story of American progress on the racial front—one that began with Rosa Parks's defiant act in Montgomery, Alabama, included the March on Washington, and resulted in the passage of the Voting Rights Act of 1964 and the Civil Rights Act of 1965.

It seemed appropriate that Reagan would invoke a poet such as Whittier on this occasion. Walt Whitman would have been a better fit for King, but Whitman's *Democratic Vistas* posed a significant challenge to Reagan's act of disremembering. "We have frequently printed the word Democracy," Whitman declared. "Yet I cannot too often repeat that it is a word the real gist of which still sleeps, quite unawakened, notwithstanding the resonance and the many angry tempests out of which its syllables have come, from pen or tongue." Whittier offered, instead, a template for imagining America's distinctiveness in its own idiom without the worry about sleepwalkers.

This was Reagan's strength. He had mastered the rhetoric of America's exceptionalism, boundless and unfettered, and he often engaged in a retelling of America's beginnings, weaving a creation myth about our national journey to perfection.

King's holiday became an occasion to affirm this vision of the country and to express faith in our promised future. Reagan said:

> *Now our nation has decided to honor Dr. Martin Luther King Jr. by setting aside a day each year to remember him and the just cause he stood for. We've made historic strides since Rosa Parks refused to go to the back of the bus. As a democratic people, we can take pride in the knowledge that we Americans recognized a grave injustice and took action to correct it. And we should remember that in far too many countries, people like Dr. King never have the opportunity to speak out at all.*

There's so much that's troubling about even this short excerpt. First, Reagan brilliantly drafted King's sacrifice and all of those who participated in the civil rights movement into a broader and persistent American narrative: that sense of our nation, no matter its shortcomings, as a singular place where liberty, equality, and individuality flourish under the watchful eyes of God. As he concluded his remarks, Reagan echoed the words of Samuel Francis Smith's "My Country, 'Tis of Thee," words King colored a deep shade of blue in the "I Have a Dream" speech: "All of God's children will be able to sing with new meaning," Reagan said, "land where my fathers died, land of the pilgrim's pride, from every mountainside, let freedom ring." With these words, Reagan ushered King into our national pantheon. He was now a true patriot—an exemplar of the American Idea, not a communist sympathizer.

Reagan's remarks in the Rose Garden also subtly reaffirmed the idea of the American people as white. When he said, "*we Americans* recognized a grave injustice" and corrected it, who are the "we" here? After all, black people had recognized the injustice a long time before Dr. King showed up. And as governor of California, Reagan was on the front lines resisting the demands of the black freedom struggle. Was his "we" the "silent majority" of the southern strategy—those who felt overrun by the demands of the civil rights movement? "The Forgotten Americans" or "Middle America" who clamored for law and order, who started a tax revolt to deny support of entitlements to lazy, would-be criminals? This idea of America appealed to white resentment.

And then we have the last line, which really kills me: the very fact that "people like Dr. King," unlike Nelson Mandela in South Africa, were able to speak at all stood as evidence of America's preeminence. For that opportunity alone, Reagan seemed to suggest, African Americans should be grateful!

After Reagan finished speaking, those in attendance began spontaneously, and somewhat tentatively, to sing "We Shall Overcome." Their nervousness spoke volumes.

With this particular embrace of the King holiday, Reagan put the final nail in a coffin for King that conservatives had been building since his death, part of a deliberate pattern that defined modern conservative approaches to the issue of race in America. In a letter in response to King's assassination, penned in 1968, Young Americans for Freedom, a leading conservative group whose youthful members would go on to play important roles in the presidencies of Ronald Reagan, George H. W. Bush, and George W. Bush, questioned King's approach to civil rights and his emphasis on race and direct action:

> *If the law can be disregarded, and if a lawbreaker can receive a Nobel Peace Prize and White House recognition, then why should the law be respected by the man in the street? If the government can loot by force, then why should people, conditioned to handouts by Dr. King's philosophy, use the intermediary of government? Why not loot directly? . . . The tragedy is that the stupid legislation continues, and government refuses to seek solutions to poverty and race relations within the private sector.*

Though King was barely in the ground, conservatives used these ideas to kill his radical vision: law and order, and shiftless, lazy black folk looking for handouts. They also contrasted the social engineering of big government with that of private-sector innovation and competition.

This wasn't your old-fashioned racism. Now the people who had once declared the importance of racial distinctions and an explicit commitment to white supremacy embraced a lesson they found in King himself: true justice was color-blind. As the historian Daniel T. Rodgers notes in his book *The Age of Fracture*,

> *What conservatives wanted now was not a restoration of the pre-Brown social order with its memories, customs, institutions, and*

rules of racial place and etiquette. They did not want history re-stored, or even remembered. What conservatives wanted now, they insisted, was a common, equal playing field and judgment on the basis of individual merit alone.

This shift in emphasis involved an appropriation of the language of the civil rights movement by conservatives. King's "I Have a Dream" speech became an important resource in this effort. What stood out for conservatives was not his rejection of the political tools that preserved the value gap; rather, it was King's dream of a day when all Americans would be "judged not by the color of their skin but by the content of their character." They read this to mean that individuals mattered, not the history of groups. Collective injustice gave way to cases of individual injury and demands for individual responsibility. In short, King's dream became the basis for eliminating discussion of race matters from public view.

Many conservatives used this formulation to attack certain features of the civil rights agenda. They sought to roll back busing as a remedy for segregated school districts, to dismantle affirmative action as a way to tackle generations of structural racism, to challenge minority set-asides that sought to address years of racial exclusion in the public sector, and to deny the significance of race in how voting districts were drawn. In each instance, the underlying assumption was simple: race-specific remedies amounted to a new kind of racism, and color-blindness was the solution. As the black conservative and the Reagan-appointed chairman of the United States Commission on Civil Rights Clarence M. Pendleton put it, "The new racism is like the old racism. They want to treat blacks and other minorities differently because of race. This is as bad as the old racists." The sin in Pendleton's mind is not persistent racial inequality or black misery but the category of race itself.

What matters in the end from this perspective is the tenacious idea of self-reliant individuals, people who provide for their own needs and pursue their own ambitions without government help. If racism rears its ugly head, it is not a reflection of racial habits, but of individual prejudice—prejudice that can be expressed in anti-black and anti-white attitudes. Both are *equally* abhorrent. Black people's anger and suspicion about white folk is as damaging as white racial prejudice. Ironically, white Americans can now use the language of the civil rights movement to defend their positions of privilege and to respond to what they describe as moral injury. They are the victims. Preference can also hide prejudice: "I don't hold bad racial views. I just want my child to go to the best school," they might say. This makes it damn near impossible to explain the advantages white Americans continue to have and the social harm experienced by African Americans. We end up with a society in which racism is rejected and taken for granted.

In this way, King's words aided the national process of turning a blind eye to the legacies of white supremacy and the persistence of racial inequality. For some, the holiday effectively washed our national hands clean. The ritual act of disremembering became a ritual of expiation: the sins of our racial past gave way to an emphasis on individual merit and responsibility. Racial inequality was not seen as the result of deeply ingrained habits, racist policies, or actual discrimination but, rather, as the result of a culture of pathology, which produced bad, irresponsible black people. Moreover, any attempt to call attention to race in public policy debates, to acknowledge the significance of racial and cultural differences in the public domain, was subject to claims of reverse racism or denounced as polarizing rhetoric, leaving racial habits unchecked in public deliberations. The result has been devastating: black suffering has been banished from public view on the national stage.

BILL CLINTON'S KING

Reagan's and neoconservative approaches to race set the terms for how the country addressed the issues of racial inequality in the subsequent decades. The election of Bill Clinton did little to change matters. In other words, this is not just a Republican story. By the 1990s, individual responsibility and interracial understanding (or the need for racial healing) trumped substantive engagement with persistent racial inequality.

Eighty percent of African Americans voted for Clinton in 1992; their support was largely responsible for his election to the presidency. But Clinton's approach of de-fanging those traditionally volatile issues that defined American politics for generations only deepened our national neurosis around racial matters. In 1993, from the pulpit of Mason Temple in Memphis, Tennessee—the church where King had delivered his "Mountaintop" speech—Clinton appropriated King for his own vision of race. If Reagan used the great civil rights leader's words to turn the idea of color-blindness inside out, Clinton—the man Toni Morrison had cheekily declared "America's first black president"—actually used King's words to shame black people—especially the black poor.

If [Martin Luther King] were to reappear by my side today and give us a report card on the last 25 years, what would he say? You did a good job, he would say, voting and electing people who formerly were not electable because of the color of their skin. You have more political power, and that is good. You did a good job, he would say, letting people who have the ability to do so live wherever they want to live, go wherever they want in this great country. . . . But he would say, I did not live and die to see the American family destroyed. . . . I did not live and die to see thirteen-year-old boys get automatic weapons and gun down nine-year-old boys just for the kick of it. . . . That is not what I came here to do. I fought for freedom, he would say, but not for the freedom of people to kill each other with reckless abandon, not for the freedom of children to have children and the fathers of the children walk away from them and abandon them as if they don't amount to anything. . . . My fellow Americans, he would say, I fought to stop white people from being so filled with hate that they would wreak violence on black people. I did not fight for the right of black people to murder other black people with reckless abandon.

This stuff is pretty difficult to swallow. From black-on-black violence to out-of-wedlock births, Clinton's political approach, with Dr. King's implied consent, conceded the terms of debate to conservatives. African Americans simply had to do better. King's sacrifice demanded as much. Here Clinton's King is no different from Reagan's.

Of course, African Americans constituted 15 percent of Clinton's administration appointments. At some point in his two-term presidency, an African American headed the Departments of Commerce, Energy, Labor, and Veterans Affairs. He also appointed more African American judges than any other president in U.S. history. For those folk (about 7 to 10 percent of black America) who benefited most from opening predominantly white colleges and universities to African Americans, Clinton's presidency represented an extraordinary advance. But Clinton also supported the Violent Crime Control and Law Enforcement Act of 1994, which exploited white fear to justify the expansion of punitive crime policy. As a result, more and more black people—particularly poor black people—found themselves in jail and prison. And his strategy of triangulation led to the passage of the Personal Responsibility and Work Opportunity Act of 1996. So-called welfare reform only widened the gap between the haves and the have-nots within black communities. All the while black liberal political elites, at least most of them, helped Clinton sell these policies to black voters.

The limits of Clinton's overall approach to race are best seen, along with this cruel legislation, in his "initiative on race." In 1997, he appointed a distinguished seven-member national commission headed by the esteemed historian John Hope Franklin. The commission was charged with advising the president "on matters involving race and racial reconciliation" and promoting "a constructive national dialogue to confront and work through challenging issues that surround race." Of course, conservatives dismissed the need for such a conversation at all, and others, especially on the left, worried that the president's initiative amounted to empty rhetoric. *The Nation* reported that "[t]he remedies are no longer as simple as taking down signs by water fountains—not that they ever were. A bold President would educate and lead. He or she would have to be willing to expend resources—dollars or political capital or points in the polls. But this President offers only his words, not his soul."

Despite these concerns about racial theater, the commission engaged in its work and issued its 104-page report, "One America in the 21st Century: Forging a New Future," in September of 1998, to mixed reviews. Many believed the commission failed at its assigned task; more-cynical observers said it was simply a symbolic gesture to score political points.

But what really mattered was the way Clinton framed the initiative in the first place. In his commencement address at the University of California San Diego, Clinton gave voice to a view of race that sounded a lot like conservatives' who were already misusing King's legacy. He asked, "Can we fulfill the promise of America by embracing all our citizens of all races?" I am not sure who is doing the embracing here, but for Clinton, it could not be bought. Big government or more federal spending was not the answer. Nor could this "embrace" be imposed. As Clinton said, "Power cannot compel it, technology cannot create it. This is something that can come only from the human spirit."

Clinton's view echoed Tocqueville's mistake in its insistence that racism does not fundamentally touch who we are *as* Americans—that our creed is secure and the problem rests only with ignorance and backwardness, only with the heart; he failed to acknowledge the value gap. Moreover, Clinton refused to see that habit formation is a social issue. It is a reflection of arrangements that incline us to value some things over others, and those habits stand in the background, moving us this way and that. His approach left in place the habits that distort the idea of who we are as a nation. No matter the demographics or the cultural shifts or who happens to be the president, we remain a *white* nation.

Along with his approach to race as a matter of the heart, Clinton also utilized a strategy of equivalence. He leveled the idea of racial injustice, in effect making all grievances the same no matter the particular histories, by demonstrating how *all* races trade in bad racial thinking.

> *We see a disturbing tendency to wrongly attribute to entire groups, including the white majority, the objectionable conduct of a few members. If a black American commits a crime, condemn the act. But remember that most African Americans are hardworking, law-abiding citizens. If a Latino gang member deals drugs, condemn the act. But remember the vast majority of Hispanics are responsible citizens who also deplore the scourge of drugs in our life. If white teenagers beat a young African American boy almost to death just because of his race, for God's sake condemn the act. But remember the overwhelming majority of white people will find it just as hateful.*

Clinton reinforces the idea that our race problem rests with bad people, with the loud racists among us, but not with all of us. He also ignores the specific histories that inform racist acts and talks only about racial stereotypes: all Americans, he reminds us, stereotype. Obviously this is true. But we don't all stereotype the same people in the same way and with the same effect.

Clinton hoped that his initiative would put the nation on the path to resolve its racial problems. He spoke passionately:

> *What do I really hope we will achieve as a country? If we do nothing more than talk, it will be interesting, but it won't be enough. If ten years from now people can look back and see that this year of honest dialogue and concerted action helped to lift the heavy burden of race from our children's future, we will have given a precious gift to America.*

How should we read Clinton's language here? What might he mean when he says "lift the heavy burden of race from our children's future"? Here Clinton's vision converged with that of Ronald Reagan. Reagan praised Dr. King for enabling Americans to step outside of the shadow of racism. This meant, at least for those who bought into Reagan's vision, that as a nation we had to leave behind race, because in governmental and social matters we were *all* Americans. As Clinton urged white Americans to see the relevance of his race initiative to their lives (the fact that he had to do so speaks volumes about how race works in the United States), he spoke these words:

> *I believe white Americans have just as much to gain as anybody else from being a part of this endeavor, much to gain from an America where we finally take responsibility for all our children so that they, at last, can be judged as Martin Luther King hoped, not by the color of their skin but by the content of their character.*

Here the idea of racial reconciliation joins seamlessly with the vision of race outlined by Reagan and others. The white man's burden now becomes lifting the burden of race. Clinton states as much at the end of his address: "That is the unfinished work of our time, to lift the burden of race and redeem the promise of America."

When Dr. King stood on the steps of the Lincoln Memorial he methodically laid out the challenges before the nation. As he reached the end of the speech, Mahalia Jackson, his favorite gospel singer, shouted out, "Tell 'em 'bout the dream, Martin." It was a prophetic beckoning. She wanted him to give voice to the power of the imagination: that one day black people, in this country, could be the human beings God called us to be. This was not a vision consonant with the white fantasy of ridding the nation of the problem of black people by making us invisible. It was something much more. King wanted us to become a democracy released from the burdens of white supremacy. Sadly, for so many now and in the hands of a certain few like Reagan and Clinton, Dr. King's words have become an instrument of the tragedy of America. Like vultures (and African Americans have joined in the feast) we have picked clean his bones, such that his powerful dream confirms the illusion of our national innocence and keeps us sleepwalking while black America withers.

CHAPTER SIX

BETWEEN TWO WORLDS

S hani Smith lives in Calumet Heights on the Southeast Side of Chicago. It is a relatively small African American community nestled between Pill Hill and Marynook, two long-standing middle-class black neighborhoods. She lives in the house she grew up in, a gorgeous redbrick Georgian. Her grandmother, Lucille Carr Buie, bought the house with money she earned "working, as she used to say, in white people's kitchens scrubbing floors [and] cooking their meals." Her grandmother was part of the second wave of migration from the South, when between 1940 and 1970 some 4.2 million black people left for a better life. She worked hard and saved her money to put a down payment on a home in 1967, because "she didn't want her grandchildren to grow up in the projects. She always wanted her family to have a house to stay in."

Now Shani owns the home where her grandmother, after three heart attacks and a battle with Alzheimer's, died. But she lost her job, and faces the possibility of foreclosure. "Everything was, you know, kind of crumbling around me at once. My aunt had taken out a loan on the house, and it had fallen to predatory lenders . . . And once that loan became too much for her, of course, the home was going into foreclosure." Like Christine Frazer and Patricia Hill, her loan passed from one company to the next—first Fremont, then to Litton, and finally to Ocwen.

Federal programs didn't help. "It was just a crazy little web in this maze of these little games they wanted to play with the housing."

Shani spoke passionately about the work she has been doing to fight the banks and to save her family's home. She joined up with other community leaders and grassroots organizations and "learned that it was the collective voices of people coming together . . . that could make a difference in this fight." She became chair of Liberate the Southside, a group of South Side and South Suburban residents who wanted to take back their neighborhoods, once vibrant communities now filled with vacant and boarded-up homes that attracted crime. "There are more vacant homes than there are homeless families!" she declared on the group's website. The organization reclaims abandoned properties and fixes them up for people who need a place to live. Shani's sister, Tene, and her kids were the first family to reclaim a foreclosed property in Calumet Heights.

As Shani talked about her organizing work and described her meetings with elected officials and the struggle to keep her home, she also spoke of a sense of loss—that the community she so loved was being ravaged by unbridled greed and by time. People like her grandmother and aunt were dying. And, in a lot of cases, "the children or the grandchildren, they're not interested in maintaining the property." Beneath the passion in her voice was the sound of lament with a hint of nostalgia. For her, something fundamental, not just the boarded-up houses, had changed.

"We don't know each other. We don't know the kids, you know? When I was coming up it was pretty much that. If you did something down on Eighty-seventh Street, your mother knew it before you got home. Because Mrs. Pearl or Mrs. Jackson or Mr. Monroe, you know, these were the folks calling your mom. 'Girl, your baby was down there fighting some other little girl on the bike.' We knew each other's kids. We knew who was coming in and out of the community." A sense of connection—of linked fate—seemed to be broken. And this was related to the loss of black institutions in the community. Places where people hung out and got to know one another, watched each other's children grow up, where people worked together to respond to the problems of their community—these places have faded. For Shani, the quality of life she remembers has also disappeared. As she put it, something has been "lost in translation."

"You had Soul Queen. That building has been for sale for years. And then you had Queen of the Sea, which sat on the intersection of Eighty-seventh and Stony Island. You also had the record store. Was it Metro Music on Fifth Street? These were the businesses that defined the community that have since gone and now you have Kenwood Liquors!" Not quite a ghost town, but definitely not the vibrant neighborhood she remembers.

What Shani describes isn't unique to her or to Calumet Heights. Black communities all across America are struggling. People have lost their homes. Businesses have shuttered their doors. Municipal budgets have been slashed. And black institutions, once robust places for black civic life, are withering on the vine. Folk are left with the shards of shattered communities. This is certainly not the "promised land" Dr. King dreamed of. In fact, black America is dying.

Let's admit right up front that the very idea of "black America" is a bit tricky. My use of the phrase suggests two possible meanings: First, the collective group of black Americans as it exists today. And second, the set of institutions that have traditionally served as the foundations of black communities in America since the early nineteenth century.

It's the first meaning that people tend to get hung up on, and with good reason. The phrase *black America* tends to suggest a monolithic bloc of people with a common history and a shared set of interests and motivations. This view tends to erase individual differences among black people, as if we're all alike. And this fact leads some, even given the sense of collective vulnerability, to question whether black people are "one" people at all.

For example, Charles Johnson, an African American novelist who wrote an influential essay titled "The End of the Black American Narrative," believes the idea and story of Black America makes little sense when confronted with all the internal differences within black communities. Rich, middle-class, and poor African Americans, and ethnic differences as a result of black immigration from the West Indies and Africa, challenge any appeal to one grand story about the journey of black people in this country—particularly a story based on the prevalence of white racism. For Johnson, "the specific conflict of this narrative reached its dramatic climax in 1963 in Birmingham, Alabama, and at the breathtaking March on Washington; its resolution arrived in 1965." We now live in different times, he claims, with different challenges, and in desperate need for new and better stories to account for the distinctiveness of our current lives.

The hip-hop artist and producer Pharrell Williams agrees, but he takes it one step further. In an interview with Oprah Winfrey, he talked about what he calls the "New Black." "The New Black doesn't blame other races for our issues. The New Black dreams and realizes that it's not pigmentation; it's a mentality. And it's either going to work for you, or it's going to work against you. And you've got to pick the side you're gonna be on." For Pharrell and Johnson, an idea of black America that overemphasizes racism or erases our individual differences fails us.

It's certainly the case that class complicates how we think about black America. In a 2007 study on race by the Pew Research Center, 61 percent of African American respondents said they believed there was a substantive difference in the values between the black middle class and the black poor. That same study reported a startling rate of African

Americans, 37 percent, who no longer believe that African Americans can be considered a single race. Many of the respondents who held this view were members of the black working poor or the black middle class, those who earned between $30,000 and $100,000 a year. But those African Americans earning more than $100,000 continue to hold the view that "blacks can still be thought of as a single race because they have so much in common."

Ethnic diversity undermines any easy idea of black America. The 1965 Hart-Cellar Immigration Act, which eliminated country-specific quotas on immigration, resulted in an influx of people from the Anglophone Caribbean. Between 1960 and 1984, more than 600,000 immigrants from places like Jamaica and Trinidad made their way to the United States. They were joined by more than 140,000 Haitian immigrants. Between 2000 and 2010 the African foreign-born population nearly doubled in size, to 1.6 million people. These are people with no personal connection to the legacy of slavery or Jim Crow segregation in the South. Their identities are not bound up with the history of race in this country, yet they were and are considered black.

I am not suggesting here that black people don't have group interests. But certain assumptions that informed the politics of the Black Power movement of the 1960s and 1970s—for example, that black people ought to share political purposes because they are black—strike me as naïve at best and politically dangerous at worst. In some ways, they assume that black people aren't political at all, that we're just hardwired to hold certain positions, as if they are encoded in our genes and evident in our skin pigment. To believe such a thing is to throw democratic politics out the window.

We also have to understand that some black people may act in ways that are not in the interest of other, more vulnerable black people. The 2007 Pew study demonstrated that most black folk aren't thinking about community in the same way. The top 1 percent of African Americans who hold on to ideas of black community often do so to leverage that idea for individual gain. They want a piece of the economic pie.

Let me put it this way: We have witnessed forty years of economic expansion among African Americans—even with the devastation of the Great Black Depression. We have seen the emergence of the black 1 percent, people like Kenneth Chenault and Oprah Winfrey. But the fact that we now have a few more rich black people doesn't mean that the majority are better off. In fact, in the time we've witnessed the growth of the black 1 percent, we have also seen the rise of mass incarceration, increased poverty, the reversal of gains in black homeownership, and an expansion of the black poor. Creating more black millionaires, as Robert L. Johnson, the founder of BET, wants to do, matters only if you subscribe to a kind of racial trickle-down economics: give rich black people more access to capital and that will help poor black people. If you believe that, I have a bridge in Brooklyn I want to sell you.

To be sure, the idea of black America has fragmented in the face of what I have just described. But I would argue nevertheless that there is still something called black America. It is made up of all those black people who identify themselves as a part of black America and its institutions. This may seem a bit circular, so let me explain what I mean.

There is a particular way race works in this country that is tied to how our people are seen and interpreted. If you have dark skin, no matter where you're from or what language you speak, you are more than likely treated as a black person. And if your appearance is ambiguous, people will try to figure out how to racially classify you. Now, we know that race is highly problematic—that the concept doesn't pass scientific muster. But we also know that in the history of this country certain people are seen as black and others are not. As W. E. B. Du Bois noted in his 1940 autobiography, *Dusk of Dawn,* the black person is one "who must ride the Jim Crow car in Georgia." In our time, black people are the ones who are stopped and frisked. In other words, black people are singled out for a certain kind of treatment in this country precisely because they are black. It is not a simple matter of how they choose to identify.

Now, *black Americans* are those people who are seen and interpreted as black *and* self-identify as black American. Here choice matters. In this sense, they understand themselves in terms of a particular history of race in this country (a history that has always included black people from other parts of the world), as individuals in association with other people who share that history, and as participants in cultural expressions and institutions bound up with that history. And this means that you may have some people who are identified as black but who do not self-identify as black American (for example, those who prefer to see themselves as Nigerian or Jamaican or just plain ol' American). So black Americans are the folks, and I include myself among them, who trace their self-understanding back to the amazing life built in the United States in the light of a society committed to the belief that white people just matter more.

This brings me to the second sense of black America: those institutions that have traditionally served as the foundation of black communities in the United States. Because of white supremacy in this country, black Americans have had to build institutions that both cultivated their civic capacities and served as a space to transmit values that opposed the value gap. Institutions like black churches emerged in the nineteenth century because of the exclusion of black Christians in predominantly white denominations (they had to sit in what were called "nigger pews," had to receive Communion last, and were not allowed to bury their dead in church cemeteries), but also because of a desire to build independent black communities.

Black churches, social clubs, schools and colleges, newspapers, masonic orders, and fraternal and sororal organizations—this broad associational life of Black America—served as the life force of communities under continuous racial assault. They provided services in lieu of the government's failure to extend the full benefits of citizenship to black people. When white schools refused to educate black children, we took on the task ourselves. When white newspapers barely covered the news in our communities or around the black world (or did so with extreme prejudice), we created news sources that helped imagine a national community across region and class. These institutions, along with informal spaces of leisure and play—the places where we danced, played cards, told jokes, and enjoyed the beauty of living a life together—not only helped black Americans to survive this racist country. They also gave us the courage to fight back.

Think about how important these institutions were to the black freedom struggle of the mid–twentieth century. Charles Hamilton Houston and his cadre of black lawyers at Howard University devised the strategy to litigate *Brown v. Board of Education*. This could not have happened at Harvard Law School. It was black students at North Carolina Agricultural and Technical State University, not at Duke University or the University of North Carolina at Chapel Hill, who decided to hold a sit-in at a Woolworth counter in Greensboro, and hundreds of other students at historically black colleges and universities across the South joined them and radicalized the civil rights movement. Black churches offered networks of interconnection across communities and states that enabled massive mobilization of people and resources to challenge racial segregation throughout the South. These institutions reflected the dreams and aspirations of black America.

Each of these institutions afforded African Americans spaces to deliberate, to think, to organize—to breathe. They are (or were) key sites for black democratic life, especially in a country where black lives aren't as valued as other people's lives. They provided the elbow room to challenge white supremacy. But more than that, they comprised a safety net or backstop for black Americans living in a society defined by the value gap—a kind of hedge against believing that we were in fact what white people said we were.

But now they are dying. The powerful black press is a shell of what it once was. Many historically black colleges and universities (HBCUs)— traditional incubators of black creativity and leadership—can barely keep their doors open. Even black churches, particularly those committed to a gospel of money, appear to have lost their way. They seem more concerned about wealth than justice.

Some would have us believe that this is the natural consequence of the end of the civil rights journey. We're now full-fledged Americans, "bowling alone" like everyone else. But I believe the loss of black institutions is troubling because black people still need them. America still needs them. Without these organizations and the forms of black politics they facilitate by providing what social scientists call "free spaces"— spaces where folks learn self-respect, public skills, and the value of civic engagement—we lose one of the crucial ways to close the value gap. These institutions enable a political vision of American democracy without white supremacy.

We should think of the problem in this way: we are between worlds. The dynamics of the current moment are not the same as those of previous moments. In a sense, Shani was right. Something has been lost in translation. We often find ourselves reaching for political language and strategies developed under one set of conditions (primarily that of the civil rights and Black Power movements of the 1960s and 1970s) to speak to circumstances that result from another set of conditions transformed by economic and political forces. Older strategies often assume a troublesome notion of collective black interests. But easy appeals to black identity don't work in the face of class, gender, sexual, and ethnic differences within black communities. They often do more harm than good. As Toni Morrison says in *Song of Solomon,* "Wanna fly, you got to give up the shit that weighs you down."

It's as if we're walking a tightrope toward a new idea of black America and we're not across the wire yet. But the places where we started are unraveling—it's all coming undone, and we're still on the rope. We know we haven't reached the other side, some post-racial utopia. That illusion has been shattered by events like Michael Brown's death, the tragic massacre in Charleston, South Carolina, and the Great Black Depression. Racial inequality continues to cut short the lives, livelihoods, and opportunities of black people in this country. Black people are still subject to premature death. Black America continues to bear the brunt of a society predicated on the value gap, except we now say we're color-blind, and the black institutions that once served as important gathering spaces to challenge that view are collapsing. We're even more vulnerable now—economically and politically.

So here is the problem: we have to let go of old, limiting ideas of black community and black politics *and* hold on to certain institutional spaces that help us respond to the fact that we are still collectively at risk. If we don't, what will provide the guarantees that these institutions once provided for a people who received no guarantees elsewhere?

The quality of life in black neighborhoods has changed dramatically since the 1960s. The steady loss of jobs, decades of government neglect, and deepening class divisions within black America have left certain black communities profoundly isolated. In the first chapter of this book, I referred to these communities as *opportunity deserts*—places where entire groups of people are considered disposable. It is in neighborhoods like these that we see most clearly the erosion of black institutional life. For years, social scientists have suggested that increasing economic inequality is reflected in civic life. People simply check out, and rightly so. They are too busy trying to put food on the table, keep a roof over their heads, and avoid landing in jail or prison thanks to the aggressive police presence in their communities.

We see the greatest decline in civic participation in black institutions among African Americans with the lowest education levels. People who live in opportunity deserts are less likely to attend church or join some other civic group. They are institutionally rudderless, lacking the "free spaces" to imagine their lives differently.

But their lack of participation isn't the only problem. Black institutions themselves (both locally and nationally) are falling apart. Their presence as places to aspire to attend (like black colleges) or as sanctuaries for the soul (like churches) diminishes daily.

Once-venerable institutions now stand on the brink of collapse or have shifted their primary focus away from neighborhoods and social justice. Many historically black colleges and universities, for example, face tremendous financial hardships (black banks, bookstores, museums, and theater companies are struggling as well). Five HBCUs have closed over the past twenty years. In the 1970s these institutions educated between 75 and 85 percent of African Americans in higher education. Today, only 9 percent of black students attend HBCUs, yet even with these small numbers, HBCUs graduate nearly 20 percent of all African Americans who earn undergraduate degrees. They produce more than 50 percent of black professionals and teachers today. So even as they struggle to stay open, HBCUs continue to show that they are uniquely committed to educating and training African Americans.

Darien Pollock is a recent graduate of Morehouse College, the all-male black school in Atlanta, Georgia (and my alma mater). He was a finalist for the Rhodes Scholarship and is currently enrolled in a Ph.D. program in philosophy at Harvard University. Darien is from Marianna, Florida, a small town with inner-city problems (unemployment, drug addiction, close to 30 percent of the population living below the poverty line). Because of family troubles, his grandparents, owners of a small mom-and-pop store, took on the task of raising him and his twin brother (who attended Morehouse as a Gates scholar). His grandmother made them toe the line and insisted, although she couldn't read well, that books would be the boys' ticket out of the slums of the South.

"She told us that you can never do enough." Darien said. "You always have to be two times better than white people."

Darien learned of Morehouse after reading a small article about one of its most famous alums, Dr. Martin Luther King Jr. He decided to visit the school. "What captured me about Morehouse was the setting. Just seeing black men doing something important," he told me. "Whether it was singing in the glee club; whether it was wearing suits to interview for some big internship. As soon as I got on campus, I saw that and I was like, 'Wow, why don't I know about this?'" He turned down the basketball scholarships and attended Morehouse instead.

Those years at school were transformative for Darien. He encountered black students who had graduated from elite boarding schools, people who had read Ernest Hemingway and Immanuel Kant. People and books he had never encountered before. He had to work hard to catch up academically, and at first he felt completely out of place. As he put it, "I felt more like an immigrant than a black person." Being poor at Morehouse was tantamount to "being a transfer student from Gambia." But Morehouse gave Darien room to discover who he was and who he aspired to be among other black men. It allowed him to see himself "within the spectrum of blackness" without having to navigate the value gap. In fact, everything about Morehouse told him that the value gap was a lie.

"Morehouse provided a space where you get to see who you are within the spectrum of blackness. The reason why that's important is because when you go into spaces like Princeton [or] Harvard you get to come in there with a type of confidence that I'm a black man, but that's not all that I am."

Morehouse allowed him to be. His identity wasn't reducible to being black. But being black wasn't devalued, either. He was able to learn and grow in an environment that repeatedly told him, even when he struggled with his own socio-economic position, that he mattered. This isn't always the case at predominantly white schools.

A colleague of mine at Princeton told me of a student who cried in her office. He was a senior and he felt like the school's racial climate was closing in on him and he couldn't take it anymore. In the spring term, Princeton students had organized protests in response to the death of Eric Garner and Michael Brown. Those who participated in the demonstrations linked that violence to what they described as the daily microaggressions they experienced at Princeton. From their perspective, the university seemed indifferent to the death of Garner and Brown, therefore indifferent to their experiences at the school. The student told my colleague that he had no place of refuge. He said, "At least you guys can go home and get away. We can't. We have to go back to our rooms with them. We have to eat in the dining halls. Attend class. There is no place to go." Everywhere he turned, he confronted an environment that wasn't nurturing and affirming—that didn't seem to care about him. He simply had to suck it up and "be black" in the way dictated by the value gap.

In spite of the value of places like Morehouse, HBCUs are struggling. In some ways, this state of affairs reflects choices in the market. Some African American students now have more opportunities to attend elite, predominantly white institutions. Schools like Princeton and Harvard offer generous financial aid packages without loans, and HBCUs, with their small endowments, can't compete. Moreover, African American academics have more options. Institutions once closed to black Ph.D.s offer more opportunities with better salaries and more resources to support individual research. It used to be the case that black students and black academics were the captured population of HBCUs. They couldn't go elsewhere. But now the competition is more intense.

HBCUs may be losing some of the top black students to elite white institutions, but they still play a crucial role for the many students who can't get into these elite schools. A good thing about the elimination of racial barriers in American higher education is that more black students could go to places like Princeton or Williams College and end up with top jobs, even become president of the United States. But it's not solving the real problem to simply shave off the top 10 percent of black students and say, okay, the doors are now open to these folks.

We have to get everyone else across the tightrope too.

Darien needed Morehouse. The school offered him a platform to make good on the talents that a place like Marianna, Florida, conspired to snuff out. How can we let these kinds of institutions die when only the most successful black people have true access to mainstream white institutions?

Matters have only gotten worse with recent federal policy. The Obama administration changed the standards for Parent PLUS loans in 2011. Borrowers could not have any accounts more than 90 days late, or any foreclosures, wage garnishments, or defaults within the last five years. This requirement was passed just three years after the economic disaster of 2008.

Predictably, the new rule change devastated black colleges. Some lost as much as 20 percent of their student body. In the academic year of 2012–13, the United Negro College Fund reported that "the number of students attending HBCUs with Parent PLUS loans dropped by 45 percent, or more than 17,000 students." Already-tight budgets were hit. Over 80 percent of the budgets of HBCUs comes from financial aid. Institutions scrambled to make up the shortfall. Some, like Morehouse, furloughed faculty. After intense criticism, the White House changed the policy, but the damage had already been done for many black students.

President Obama also announced a plan to offer two years of free tuition to qualified students attending community colleges. But his administration did not consider the effects of the policy on HBCUs. Many HBCUs compete with community colleges for students, and the Obama administration put its thumb on the scale by not extending free tuition for the first two years to attend public HBCUs. In effect, he incentivized students to go elsewhere.

In a February 2015 meeting with the Congressional Black Caucus, several representatives stated that President Obama made his feelings about HBCUs quite clear. Representative Hank Johnson of Georgia, a graduate of Clark Atlanta University, put it this way: "[Obama] said that there were some HBCUs that were not good at graduating students and if they did not improve they'd have to go by the wayside." He didn't seem to care about the complicated relationship between finances and graduation rates at HBCUs—that people took time off to work to earn money to pay for school or they dropped out because the money ran out. Johnson continued, "In other words, he didn't show much empathy for struggling HBCUs. It was like, 'Show me the numbers, and if the numbers aren't where they need to be, that's it.' It was a somewhat callous view of the unique niche HBCUs fill."

These institutions once housed the brain trust of black America, and despite the conservative politics that often informed how they were run, the schools afforded black students and intellectuals the safe space to confront the enormous challenges facing black America. But HBCUs now face the fate of black newspapers. Once the names of the *Pittsburgh Courier* and the *Chicago Defender* and the Black Associated Press had national standing. African Americans throughout the country turned to newspapers and newswires like these for information about black America and about the black world at large. These papers enabled an imagined community—a sense of connection with other black people across the country who faced similar trials and tribulations. But the black freedom struggle of the 1960s sealed the fate of these news outlets. Their influence waned as doors once closed opened and black reporters migrated to mainstream print media and black readers followed them.

This isn't necessarily a bad thing. I am not longing for the days of segregated black communities with segregated black institutions. But the fact is that these institutions played vital roles in black communities, and the question of what happened once they disappeared looms large for communities still under siege. The demise of black newspapers, for example, represented the beginning of the contraction of formal places where African Americans could think with one another about issues confronting our communities. It was in the pages of black newspapers that African Americans could read in-depth analysis of debates in Congress. The newspapers chronicled the Great Migration and urged African Americans in the South to leave the region with advertisements for work and a better life. You can read the letters to the editor written to the *Chicago Defender* attesting to the role the newspaper played in the lives of migrants seeking a better life.

Now Black Twitter (thousands of people who tweet regularly about issues of race in the news and popular culture) and Facebook offer alternative sites for the work that black newspapers once provided. Without black social media, the cases of Trayvon Martin and Marissa Alexander would have never gotten any traction. Martin, for example, was killed on February 26, 2012. Two weeks later, the Sanford police turned over the case to the state. But Zimmerman wasn't arrested until six weeks after that. It was only after outrage rose on Twitter and Facebook that the story garnered national attention. These platforms allow for a different way of imagining black community and a fascinating mode of mobilizing interests: tweets, Vine, Instagram, and trending topics on Facebook offer black public spaces in which issues facing black communities can circulate at the blink of an eye or with 140 characters.

We now face a question about the fate of HBCUs. Given the role these institutions have played in black America—as incubators for black intellectual creativity and black student activism—what will now stand as the primary space for intellectual work around black communities and housing, chronic unemployment, and mass incarceration? Of course, the top HBCUs will remain with us for the foreseeable future. Spelman is secure. Morehouse, Howard, Tuskegee, and Hampton have experienced rough patches, but their brands ensure their doors will remain open. But places like Morris Brown College in Atlanta are the walking dead (today the college enrolls only 35 students; 107 students were enrolled at the time of its founding in 1885). We will continue to see the trend lines of more and more black students attending and black academics teaching at predominantly white institutions. Perhaps the function of HBCUs will now rest in the hands of those of us who teach African American studies in these places? We have the resources, the students, and the institutional infrastructure to offer space to think critically about the challenges confronting black America. But who knows? Everything is changing, and until we have a better sense of what that change looks like, HBCUs are necessary—if not vital.

In 2014, the Koch brothers gave the United Negro College Fund $25 million. Michael Lomax, the fund's president and CEO, was unapologetic in accepting the gift. "My job is to raise money and help kids go to and complete college," he said. The majority of the gift will go directly to scholarships and to the 37 UNCF member colleges and universities. It is a much-needed infusion of support for institutions struggling to keep their doors open. But the Koch brothers are the face and financial backing of conservative policies that have devastated black communities throughout this country. You might as well accept money from the Klan.

This business with UNCF is a far cry from the pride I felt when I watched as a child the UNCF telethon hosted by the late Lou Rawls. "A mind is a terrible thing to waste," he used to say in his sultry baritone. And a soul is a terrible thing to sell. But what are we to do?

Black colleges and universities need the money. And if help doesn't come soon, many will have to close their doors for good. What will happen then? Who will provide the space for students and intellectuals to tackle the issues confronting black America *without qualification*—without the need to justify its worthiness as a topic of consideration? Who will provide the breathing room for the next playwrights, novelists, and poets to dare to be unabashedly black—without the burden of navigating the value gap—in their aesthetic choices and in their identification with the traditions that inform their unique voices? All of these things are still needed. We are still collectively vulnerable. If HBCUs are going to go by the wayside we should at least know, given the precarious place of black folk in this country, what—if anything—will take their place.

Coretta Scott King died in 2006 of complications from ovarian cancer. Her funeral was an extravagant affair. More than 15,000 people attended, including four presidents. Politics mixed with grief during a six-hour service as people paid tribute in word and song to the "first lady of black America."

But the funeral was shrouded in controversy. Many noted the absence of her longtime friend Harry Belafonte, and some were distraught that the funeral was not held at Dr. King's Ebenezer Baptist Church in Atlanta. Instead the service took place at New Birth Missionary Baptist Church, a large congregation of more than 25,000 members situated on a 250-acre campus in Lithonia, Georgia, and pastored by the charismatic and controversial Bishop Eddie Long. With its opulent sanctuary, 6,100 amphitheater seats, four large video screens, and orchestra pit,

New Birth epitomized a different kind of black church from the one associated with the life of Mrs. King and her famous husband.

Bernice King, an elder at New Birth, insisted the funeral be held there. As she eulogized her mother, she said,

> *You are not sitting in this church just because it was logical to be here. . . . Should we have it at the civic center? Should we have it at New Birth? . . . And I said, God, why, why here? He said because it's time for the world to be born again. It's time for a New Birth. . . . God is not looking for a Martin Luther King or Coretta Scott King. The old has passed away; there is a new order that is emerging.*

For her, Bishop Long had inherited the mantle of Dr. King's and her mother's legacy. The going-home service of her mother was the occasion to announce that fact to the world.

She had said as much two years earlier. In 2004, Long led a march to the tomb of Dr. King in protest of gay marriage and Bernice King lit a torch from the eternal flame of her father's burial site, passing it to Long as a kind of symbolic coronation. The irony wasn't lost on many who observed the spectacle: a march against same-sex marriage occasioned a moment to disremember Dr. King, with his daughter profoundly complicit in it all.

Since those lofty days, Bishop Long has fallen to remarkable lows. In 2010, two young men filed lawsuits accusing him of using his position to coerce them into sexual relationships. Bernice King has left the church. Long is no longer considered (as if he ever was) the heir to Dr. King's legacy. But the fall of Bishop Long should not be seen as an isolated instance of a corrupt and hypocritical preacher. The theology and business model of New Birth wasn't unique to him. It has spread like a virus throughout black Christendom, transforming the role and function of black churches from the prophetic spaces we associate with the civil rights movement, which provided resources for the most vulnerable in our communities and helped challenge white supremacy, to profit centers in the name of God.

We have witnessed over the past few decades the disappearance of the neighborhood church in cities around the country, driven largely by the rapid suburbanization of the black middle class. As churches embraced growth plans that involved following these congregants to the suburbs, they left poor communities behind. And if the church stayed in the city, its members more than likely drove in from the surrounding suburbs. They no longer lived in the neighborhood.

The shift in location affected the social function of black churches in poor neighborhoods. What happens to the church as a hub of communal life (from food banks to job training to places for local neighborhood meetings) when most of the people who attend the church don't live in the neighborhood or the church has relocated to some sprawling campus like a religious version of Walmart or Home Depot? In effect, communities left behind lose a vital institutional space that connects with their everyday lives.

Moreover, the popularity of what has been called prosperity gospel, a view that God wills that those who are born again be materially wealthy (a view Bishop Long adapted), has greatly affected how some black churches understand the gospel and its relation to questions of justice. Creflo Dollar, pastor of the World Changers Church International and the preacher who asked his members to buy him a $65 million jet, illustrates this view when he says:

Many people think poverty and prosperity are words that only describe the state of one's finances; however, these terms involve much more than that. The Bible describes poverty, or being poor, as being insufficient in any area of life. Prosperity is abundance in every area of life. Prosperity is a result of God's blessing. And poverty is a curse, the result of disobeying God.

For Dollar and many others, wealth is a sign of God's blessing. Poverty is a sign of his punishment. What results is an understanding of the African American Christian as a "blessed entrepreneur and consumer" and the church as a place to facilitate his or her exercise of choice/blessings.

This view changes the social function of the church in that it blunts criticism of racial inequality. It short-circuits mobilization around poor communities, because wealth and aspiration for upward mobility are reduced to individual spiritual concerns. We just need to get our souls straight and the money will follow. No criticism of power. No concern about broader questions of justice. This led me to declare that the black church was dead: that the idea of the black church as a progressive institution had given way to a routine invocation of its often imagined past glories and an embrace of a gospel uniquely suited for these times. It's as if the legacy of Dr. King and the prophetic church has been eclipsed by the gospel according to Reverend Ike, the famed preacher of the 1970s, depicted by Richard Pryor as "Daddy Rich" in *Car Wash,* who was known for his ostentatious lifestyle and his gospel of health and wealth. Today Reverend Ike's approach seems to have won out among certain preachers as they have given up the prophetic church for their own material gain.

Of course, this leaves black communities all the more vulnerable. Without institutions that, in some ways, serve as buffers against economic and political forces driven by racial habits and the value gap, African Americans are subject to dangerous winds without any shelter. Matters have changed, but racial inequality persists. We still need institutions, beyond the traditional civil rights organizations, to affirm black people and facilitate grassroots organizing around issues like jobs, education, and policing—to support those who directly challenge policies and practices that deepen white supremacy's hold on our democracy. Some black churches and pastors, like Dr. Frederick D. Haynes III in Dallas, Dr. Otis Moss III in Chicago, and Dr. Leslie Callahan in Philadelphia, are doing this work. They need help.

Black churches, black colleges and universities, black workers, the black middle class, black communities in general find themselves between two worlds, one world coming undone and the other out of reach. The resources that once enabled us to think about racial progress persist now in nostalgic longings for a time passed or in invocations of a politics that doesn't quite fit the moment. People continue to march. But there are voices, young bold voices, emerging that point toward a different path. Some established black leaders attempt to silence those voices as they invoke Dr. King and profit from the business of racial advocacy. They proclaim over and over again that folks died for the right to vote while they leverage the possibility of delivering black voters to the polls for political influence and selfish gain. But poor black communities stay poor. Black unemployment remains high. We continue to lose our homes. And black institutions collapse. We don't live in a world where a lot of truly integrated institutions exist. Black institutions have simply had to disappear and black people have had to adjust to the demands of working and living in predominantly white spaces. Those who could make it across the deep divides have had to adjust. The rest of black America has seemingly been left to suffer a slow death.

What will happen if these institutions disappear altogether? What will provide us with the space to imagine ourselves differently and to courageously challenge white supremacy in this country? Or, as James Baldwin put it, "what will happen to all that beauty?"

Baldwin asked this question as he grappled with the political nature of race. Color, for him, "is not a human or a personal reality; it is a political reality." The political reality was and remains that as long as white people valued themselves more than others because they were white and refused to examine their habits and assumptions, others would have to come together, build institutions, and act politically on the basis of color. The question about the status of "all that beauty" is one about what our experiences tell us about being human, and how they offer a pathway for democracy in which the lives of black people matter as much as everyone else. As white supremacy digs in its heels, as the complexity of black identities betrays the lie that all black people are alike, and as the economic crisis continues to devastate black America, we can't help but ask "what will happen to all that beauty?" We haven't reached any kind of promised land. We stand between lands, desperately holding on as we see so many people we love fall into poverty, go off to prison, or end up in the grave.

In other words, declarations that we no longer need black America without a systematic dismantling of white supremacy amount to requests that black people commit collective suicide.

CHAPTER SEVEN

PRESIDENT OBAMA AND BLACK LIBERALS

W ho would have thought that the election of the nation's first black president would occasion the moment for this kind of crisis in black America? It is the sort of irony we usually only find in fiction. A reversal of sorts: a *black* president who presides over the dismantling of a tradition, who masterfully uses the language of black struggle in the service of Wall Street, who is lauded for his celebration of black culture and his performance of black cultural cues, but whose policies leave much to be desired. This is someone who chastises black people for eating Popeye's chicken for breakfast.

Barack Obama is, of course, not the reason we are between two worlds. But his presidency hasn't helped anything; rather, he is emblematic of the problem. We've come so far as a nation that we can elect a black man to be president of the United States, but racial inequality gets worse on his watch.

For eight years some black critics, like my friend Cornel West, have been obsessed with President Obama's failures. Much of that anger is rooted in profound disappointment and righteous outrage at the state of black America and of the country. "We ended up with a Rockefeller Republican in blackface," West said in 2012. In an interview, West, who participated in 65 campaign events for candidate Obama, put his disappointment this way:

> *This was maybe America's last chance to fight back against the greed of the Wall Street oligarchs and corporate plutocrats, to generate some serious discussion about public interest and common good that sustains any democratic experiment. . . . We are squeezing out all of the democratic juices we have. They are scapegoating the most vulnerable rather than confronting the most powerful. . . . I thought Barack Obama could have provided some way out.*

Instead Americans got more of the same.

Obama refuses to engage directly the crisis sweeping black America. When asked about the state of black unemployment or the racial dimension of the housing crisis, Obama repeatedly claims his policies will lift all boats. He held a beer summit for Harvard professor Henry Louis Gates Jr. when Cambridge police arrested him for "breaking into" his own home. He empathized with the parents of Trayvon Martin, dispatched Attorney General Eric Holder to hotbeds of racial unrest, established a commission about policing, and insisted on the rule of law in the face of protests against police brutality. But expectations that we had someone in the White House who was truly sensitive to the concerns of black communities were at best misguided or, worse, vestiges of an old way of thinking about black politics—the idea that because Obama is black, he would act in the interest of black people.

Obama was supposed to be more. He was ideally our black progressive antidote to the conservative policies of the Bush years. After the horror of Hurricane Katrina in New Orleans, as lifeless black bodies floated in toxic water and the federal response left many more to die with them, Kanye West expressed what most black people felt: "George Bush doesn't care about black people." Bush took it that West was calling him a racist. As he wrote in his book *Decision Points,* "I faced a lot of criticism as president. . . . But the suggestion that I was racist because of the response to Katrina represented an all-time low." That is not what West meant. He didn't mean Bush hated black people, or consciously thought less of them. Bush just didn't *care* about black people. He didn't really think about us.

Obama was supposed to be different. He was supposed to care about black people. When I listen to Cornel West I hear more than a strident criticism of Obama's policies. I hear bitter disappointment. And the disappointment goes beyond the president. We've been duped, and we're angry with ourselves. Many progressives "green-screened" him. We made Obama whatever we wanted him to be. If we wanted an antiwar candidate, he was it. If we wanted someone who supported universal health care he was it; someone who would challenge Wall Street, he was our guy; a candidate committed to the poor, Obama was our man. He was our political Play-Doh. And he obliged our fantasies all the way to the White House. Obama said as much in *The Audacity of Hope*: "I am new enough on the national political scene that I serve as a blank screen on which people of vastly different political stripes project their own views. As such, I am bound to disappoint some, if not all, of them." As we say back home in Mississippi, "He ain't never lied!"

We should have known better. Nothing Obama said actually confirmed the belief that he was some progressive savior. He is what he has always been.

I believe in the free market, competition, and entrepreneurship, and think no small number of government programs don't work as advertised. I wish the country had fewer lawyers and more engineers. I think America has been more often a force for good than for ill in the world; I carry few illusions about our enemies, and revere the courage and competence of our military. I reject a politics that is

*based solely on racial identity, gender identity, sexual orientation,
or victimhood generally. I think much of what ails the inner city
involves a breakdown in culture that will not be cured by money
alone, and that our values and spiritual life matter at least as much
as our GDP.*

This is Obama, and he has been remarkably consistent over these eight
years. Many progressives willfully ignored who he was, because we so
desperately wanted someone to deliver us from the political sins of our
times. That wish revealed how limited our political imaginations have
become.

For most of the twentieth century, African American politics con-
sisted of a wide range of ideologies that challenged white supremacy in this country. The kind of black liberalism informing Obama's
politics was just one option among many. In the early twentieth century, the NAACP, the National Urban League, and the National Association of Colored Women's Clubs stood alongside organizations like
Marcus Garvey's Universal Negro Improvement Association and the
National Negro Congress and the Council on African Affairs. Black
liberals struggled alongside black nationalists and Communists, people
who conceived of black political life beyond the borders of the United
States and who pushed up against any easy embrace of the belief that,
no matter our practices, America was a place committed to freedom,
equality, and the rights of every person. Black nationalists and Communists seriously questioned the American Idea. Black left activists like
Cyril Briggs, Hubert Harrison, Harry Haywood, Claudia Jones, and
Paul Robeson (names we rarely hear anymore outside of college class-
rooms) offered a radical critique of the nation, and linked that criticism
with the conditions of black and brown people around the world. They

joined with the venerable W. E. B. Du Bois, one of the founders of the NAACP, in insisting on a deeper understanding of the relationship between capitalism, white supremacy, and empire. Their presence (many were West Indian immigrants) enriched the black political landscape as they worked with and alongside black liberals to challenge white supremacy at home and abroad.

Much of this radical energy would fall victim to the Cold War and the push for consensus. In January of 1948, the U.S. attorney general, Tom Clark, made clear the stakes: "Those who do not believe in the ideology of the United States shall not be allowed to stay in the United States." McCarthyism led to the persecution of figures like Du Bois and Robeson. Du Bois was arrested as "an agent of a foreign principal" in February of 1951. At the age of 82, he was handcuffed and fingerprinted. The national media made him out to be a common criminal. Robeson lost his ability to travel abroad and to perform. He died broken and alone. The upshot was that any hint of communism or socialism shaping black politics had to be purged, and the radical elements of black political life marginalized. Black liberalism had to stand alone.

No wonder the popular story of black politics in the twentieth century begins with the founding of the NAACP; makes a brief mention of the Harlem Renaissance; documents court cases that end with the 1954 *Brown v. Board of Education* decision; and finally culminates with the civil rights movement, Dr. King's "I Have a Dream" speech in 1963, and Obama's election. It's as if nothing happened in the 1930s and 1940s of significance; as if the radical elements of the 1960s and 1970s did not matter at all.

Part of the problem has been a narrowing of what is politically possible. Over the years, the broad sweep of black political life has been winnowed down to what some take to be the only acceptable form of black politics: black liberalism. This has involved an all-out assault on our radical political imaginations; all we are left to do is "tinker" with the current system. Other forms of black politics become seen as not just unacceptable, but damaging. The Black Power movement gets reduced to an orgy of violence or a simple demand for black cultural recognition. Blotted from view are the complexities of Malcolm X, the Student Non-Violent Coordinating Committee (SNCC), and the Black Panther Party. These were people and organizations who sought to uproot white supremacy in every facet of American society. They insisted that black was beautiful and that poor black people should participate fully in the democratic process, and they challenged economic arrangements that exploited black communities. Malcolm and groups like these come to us now in movies like *The Butler* and *Selma,* where they represent an irrational, angry politics that seems completely out of bounds because it heightens white fear and fails to understand how "real" politics works. Under these conditions, how can we recall the importance of the Dodge Revolutionary Union Movement or the League of Revolutionary Black Workers, or the radicalism of the African Liberation Support Committee? These end up seeming like residual traces of bad black politics.

Truncated political imaginations give us limited political options. We imagine what's possible within a narrow band of options provided by a political philosophy that, for all intents and purposes, is bankrupt when it comes to fundamentally changing black lives. Black liberalism ends up being the only game in town. No wonder we green-screened Obama. We wanted so much more, but he was our *only* choice.

"Damn Black Liberals"

The election of Barack Obama should be understood as the logical conclusion of a form of black politics that has guided much of African American life since the dawn of the twentieth century. You can't draw a straight line from the founding of the NAACP in 1909 and the National Urban League in 1910 to Obama'a political ascendance; there are real differences between these moments and a lot happened in between. What connects them, however, is the underlying political philosophy of black liberalism: a view that takes broad-base inclusion of black people into American life as its aim without closing the value gap.

Obama's politics reflects a set of guiding principles about the role of government in our lives, and a commitment to a framework of rights and fair procedures that accord equal respect and standing to individuals. Individuals are seen as independent rational actors who are capable of "choosing their own values and ends." In this sense, Obama, like most black liberals (and here I am thinking about the likes of U.S. Senator Cory Booker, former Governor Deval Patrick of Massachusetts, Marc Morial of the National Urban League, the Reverend Al Sharpton of the National Action Network, Sherrilyn Ifill of the NAACP Legal Defense and Educational Fund), is no different from any white liberal in the country.

By liberal I don't mean someone on the political left. I simply mean that Obama adheres to a very old political tradition that can be traced back to the sixteenth century and to the likes of John Locke and John Stuart Mill. He is committed to individual rights, to relatively free markets, and to an idea of government that, all things being equal, is minimally intrusive in our individual efforts to maximize our ambitions. Most Americans, whether they are on the political left or right, are liberal in this sense. And a core set of values sits at the center of it all. Obama puts it this way:

> *The values of self-reliance and self-improvement and risk-taking. The values of drive, discipline, temperance, and hard work. The values of thrift and personal responsibility. These values are rooted in a basic optimism about life and a faith in free will—a confidence that through pluck and sweat and smarts, each of us can*

rise above the circumstances of our birth. . . . Our system of self-government and our free-market economy depend on the majority of the individual Americans adhering to these values. The legitimacy of our government and our economy depend on the degree to which these values are rewarded, which is why the values of equal opportunity and nondiscrimination complement rather than impinge on our liberty.

Obama expresses these views as a kind of consensus, which harkens back to the postwar liberal consensus of the mid–twentieth century: a common set of values that connects us and enables us, despite our differences, to hold a jointly shared vision of the country. Like Paul Ryan, he believes that these shared values—"the standards and principles that the majority of Americans deem important in their lives and in the life of the country—should be the heart of our politics."

Obama is also a certain kind of *black* liberal. Black liberals generally hold basic liberal principles, but with the understanding that white supremacy and its habits undermine their application to all Americans. These persistent racist practices require a strong central government to check the consequences of racial prejudice and violence. Think of the role of the National Guard in integrating Little Rock Central High School in 1957 or the federal marshals needed to enroll James Meredith in Ole Miss in 1961. In each instance, federal power was deployed to protect black people. White supremacy makes groups just as important as individuals, because black people as a group, no matter if they are middle class or poor, face unequal treatment because they are black.

Black liberalism ostensibly separates liberal principles from white supremacy, holding that racism distorts the American Idea. The thought here is that if African Americans were woven into the fabric of American life, that inclusion would fundamentally transform America. We can trace this idea back to the early nineteenth century in the writings of Frederick Douglass and other abolitionists. We see the formulation at work in the NAACP and other civil rights organizations of the 1940s and 1950s. And we certainly see it used throughout the civil rights movement of the 1960s. Dr. King and other movement activists repeatedly pointed out the failure of the nation to live up to its principles when it came to black people. And they invoked the idea of common American values as the basis of their criticisms.

King makes such an appeal in his famous "I Have a Dream" speech:

> *In a sense we've come to our nation's capital to cash a check. When the architects of our republic wrote the magnificent words of the Constitution and the Declaration of Independence, they were signing a promissory note to which every American was to fall heir. This note was a promise that all men, yes, black men as well as white, would be guaranteed the "unalienable rights" of "life, liberty, and the pursuit of happiness"... . Instead of honoring this sacred obligation, America has given the Negro people a bad check, a check which has come back marked insufficient funds. But we refuse to believe that the bank of justice is bankrupt. We refuse to believe that there are insufficient funds in the great vaults of opportunity of this nation.*

The underlying assumption here is that the American Idea is not inherently bad or in need of revision. *It* isn't racist. Rather, *we* are the racists and are in need of redemption. We simply need to align our practices with our stated principles and values. This view enables us to hold simultaneously that the principles of freedom and liberty are already a part of American life, while we experience, over and over again, habits and practices that suggest otherwise.

In this sense, the black liberal argument is, and always will be, an argument about America on the terms of its stated creed. The different forms of African American politics have been based on the degree to which one accepts the terms of that creed. Black nationalists reject the creed out of hand. Black socialists and Communists see it as a ruse to hide the horrors of racial capitalism. Black liberals, especially President Obama, accept the American Idea "straight, no chaser."

Different kinds of black liberals hold this view today. The Reverend Jesse Jackson and U.S. Representatives John Lewis and Maxine Waters come to mind as examples of *traditional black liberals*. These are people committed to the American Idea and to equality irrespective of the color of your skin or how much money you have. They criticize the various ways white supremacy, as individual acts of prejudice and as structural inequality, undermines democratic life in this country and they insist on robust federal protection and intervention to prevent and remedy racial discrimination. In short, traditional black liberals believe the problem rests with the gap between our ideals and our practices—a problem best resolved by government. Lewis, for example, in response to the demonstrations in Ferguson after Michael Brown's death, said on MSNBC, "My own feeling right now is that President Obama should use the authority of his office to declare martial law, federalize the Missouri National Guard to protect people as they protest." For him and other traditional liberals, the principles of fairness and egalitarianism dictate the role of government in our lives, and the idea of justice is as important as the principle of liberty. These notions, along with the core values of the country that Obama invokes, shape how traditional black liberals engage with economic, social, and racial issues.

There are also *conservative black liberals*. People like Supreme Court Justice Clarence Thomas, conservative writer Shelby Steele, and Republican presidential candidate Ben Carson hold steadfast to the American Idea and to notions of black self-reliance. Conservative black liberals laud markets and insist that racism, if it persists at all, is a matter only of individual acts of prejudice. Like traditional black liberals, they believe the problem is the gap between our ideals and our actions, but they *don't* believe government can close the gap. For them, a commitment to the values of hard work and personal responsibility ensures black progress, not a strong federal government that they think encourages dependency. In fact, in the minds of most conservative black liberals, big government does more harm than good.

Between the traditional and conservative black liberal stand the *post-black liberal.* These are people who believe in the American Idea and acknowledge the history of racism but deemphasize its current relevance, and appeal to ideas of efficient government in partnership with the private sector as a remedy for social ills. Post-black liberals recognize the legacy of racial discrimination but also insist on personal responsibility and accountability. They have a faith in markets, as conservative black liberals do, and they don't believe government has all the answers to the problems of black communities. They split the difference between traditional and conservative black liberals, as they appeal not to a totally color-blind America, but to an America in which race doesn't really matter as much. In this sense, post-black liberals are "race transcenders"— they acknowledge race only to point to the need to get beyond race.

President Obama captured the general philosophy of the post-black liberal in his speech commemorating the fiftieth anniversary of "Bloody Sunday" in Selma:

> *The Americans who crossed this bridge were not physically imposing. But they gave courage to millions. They held no elected office. But they led a nation. . . . What could be more American than what happened in this place? What could more profoundly vindicate the idea of America than plain and humble people . . . coming together to shape their country's course? What greater expression of*

faith in the American experiment than this; what greater form of patriotism is there than the belief that America is not yet finished, that we are strong enough to be self-critical, that each successive generation can look upon our imperfections and decide that it is in our power to remake this nation to more closely align with our highest ideals?

Post-black liberals at their best! Racial matters enter in as a momentary stumble on our way to a more perfect union. Here the American Idea reigns supreme (and this is true for all black liberals).

But black liberalism of whatever stripe comes with a cruel irony. The demands for racial reform dovetail all too easily with the American fantasy that black people will disappear. That vanishing act would be part of a broader idea of America, where the ugliness of past practices gives way to "a more perfect union," and where the language of national consensus limits what can be said about black suffering. Again, Obama made this move in *The Audacity of Hope* and has governed by it for two terms:

An emphasis on universal, as opposed to race-specific, programs isn't just good policy; it's also good politics. . . . Rightly or wrong, white guilt has largely exhausted itself in America; even the most fair-minded of whites, those who would genuinely like to see racial inequality ended and poverty relieved, tend to push back against suggestions of racial victimization—or race-specific claims based on the history of race discrimination in this country. . . . As a result, proposals that solely benefit minorities and dissect Americans into "us" and "them" may generate a few short-term concessions when the costs to whites aren't too high, but they can't serve as the basis for the kinds of sustained, broad-based political coalitions needed to transform America.

In other words, consensus requires that the particulars of black people's suffering are left behind. White people demand as much, because they are no longer guilty about this race stuff.

This is the vision Ralph Johnson Bunche, the noted black political scientist who received the Nobel Peace Prize in 1950, put forward in his 1949 commencement address at Fisk University:

> *The Negro graduates of Fisk University are better Americans than they are Negroes. They are Negro primarily in a negative sense. They reject that sort of treatment that deprives them of their birthright as Americans. Remove that treatment and their identification as Negroes in American society would become meaningless—at least as meaningless as it is to be of English, or French, or German, or Italian ancestry.*

On its face, this seems like a laudable goal—to be treated as an American, to be judged by the content of one's character alone. This is the hope of color-blindness. But this state of affairs requires that we leave our "identification as Negroes" at the doorstep. It also demands that we believe that being "American" is not inextricably bound to the idea that white people are valued most in this country. This denial limits the scope of black protest: all we're left to do is protest that we have failed to live up to our ideals or demand more just laws, while the value gap is left untouched. Our entrée into American society is not only contingent on the eradication of racism, but also on the disappearance of black people altogether. Black people must lose their blackness if America is to be transformed. But—of course—white people get to stay white.

This is the devastating irony that rests at the heart of black liberalism. The quest to align black freedom with the ideals of America contains within it a death warrant for black America itself. W. E. B. Du Bois saw the implication of this view in 1926. He asked, "What do we want? What is the thing we are after?"

> [I]t has a certain truth: We want to be Americans, full-fledged Americans, with all the rights of other American citizens. But is that all? Do we simply want to be Americans? Once in a while through all of us there flashes some clairvoyance, some clear idea, of what America really is. We who are dark see America in a way that Americans cannot. And seeing our country thus, are we satisfied with its present ideals?

We don't want to integrate into America as it is. We don't believe white people possess something of intrinsic value that we need or desperately want. Our aim is not to corroborate the value of whiteness by desiring its status and benefits. Something more fundamental is at stake in our claim on America (or at least it should be), and that something is deeply connected to our experiences as black people in the United States. We know what democracy can be, because we have felt viscerally what it is not.

But there is the idea, and it has been a feature of postwar American liberalism since the beginning of the Cold War, that the price of wholesale inclusion in this society is that we actively forget we are black people—that we become just Americans while white people continue to benefit from being white. The irony, of course, is that the active forgetting—the disremembering—is one of the crucial ways white supremacy in the twenty-first century sustains itself. And black liberalism has helped it stay alive.

President Obama represents the culmination of this tradition. How he engages matters of race, how he imagines black people's relation to the nation, and how he uses African American history affirm this liberal vision. In some ways, all the declarations in 2008 that we had reached the promised land revealed the deadly gambit at the heart of black liberal politics: that somehow our inclusion at the highest levels of power would finally unhook white supremacy from the nation's precious ideals and we would be free. But the price of this "freedom" was communal death in service of the illusion of racial progress.

Of course, black politics hasn't always been tethered to the American Idea. Prior to the advent of the Cold War, black activists imagined black politics in domestic *and* global terms. They envisioned the struggle of black people in America as intimately and philosophically linked to struggles of other oppressed people around the world. The American Idea was given the lie by its connection to the unfreedom enforced upon much of the globe by colonialism and imperialism. Even black liberals leveraged geopolitical matters for the benefit of African Americans at home. They argued for broad-base citizenship rights as they fought Jim Crow in the South and connected that struggle to the liberation of Africans and Asians everywhere. The anthem of "Lift Every Voice and Sing," written and composed by James Weldon Johnson and his brother, J. Rosamond Johnson, celebrated a distinctiveness that could not be contained by U.S. borders. So in the first four decades of the twentieth century, black liberals argued for the vote, insisted on self-reliance and economic independence, organized Pan-African Conferences and Congresses, and dared to imagine America on different terms. A young Du Bois, before his embrace of communism, voiced in 1903 the distinctive approach of black liberals that rejected an idea of America as a "shining city upon the hill."

> *Your country? How came it yours? Before the Pilgrims landed we were here. Here we have brought our three gifts and mingled them with yours: a gift of story and song . . . ; the gift of sweat and brawn to beat back the wilderness, conquer the soil, and lay the foundations*

of this vast economic empire two hundred years earlier than your weak hands could have done it; the third, a gift of Spirit. . . . Are not these gifts worth giving? Is not this work and striving? Would America have been America without her Negro people?

Here Du Bois insists on a different vision of the country—one that isn't predicated on the idea that America is God's chosen nation. Instead, the experiences of black people are the basis for a radical imagining of what America is and what the country might be.

Obama is not this kind of black liberal. For him, if the distinctiveness of black folk is to be mentioned at all, it is only to confirm the greatness of our country. What choices were made to yoke black liberalism to the American Idea? What happened to make post black-liberals like President Obama possible? Three historical moments set the stage for this shift and they, along with the demands for Cold War consensus, narrowed the range of black politics.

1. The Black Liberal Compact

During the hot summer days of July 1946 black women from across the country picketed the White House. The National Association of Colored Women (NACW) had recently denounced the brutal lynching of Roger and Dorothy Malcolm and George Dorsey, a World War II veteran, and his wife Mae Murray Dorsey in Walton County, Georgia. A white mob had lined up like a firing squad and riddled their bodies with bullets in the fields of Moore's Ford, so much so that "the upper parts of the bodies were scarcely recognizable." One of the women was seven months pregnant. She was shot more than sixty times. The other had her hands crushed and spine shattered by the firing squad. People heard the screams, but no one in Walton County would talk. As Walter White, the executive director of the NAACP from 1931 to 1955, noted,

"A reign of terror and fear swept over Walton County and effectively shut the mouths of both whites and Negroes."

Christine S. Smith, president of the NACW, along with 300 other women marched on the White House demanding a federal response to the horrors of lynching and "justice [for] the perpetrators of the Georgia crime." The women held the picket line for a week. At one point, as more women joined the protest, about 500 of them stormed into the Capitol. They wanted to see their senators. Their protests would be joined by others, horrified by the deaths in Monroe. The National Negro Congress led a march of more than a thousand people from Union Station to the White House to protest President Truman's relative silence regarding the violence. More than 15,000 people took to the streets in New York and another 15,000 marched to the Lincoln Memorial to demand anti-lynching legislation. Between June of 1945 and September of 1946, fifty-six black people were murdered in acts of racial violence. White southerners were killing black people (particularly black veterans) with impunity and the Truman administration refused to do anything about it.

Two different responses emerged in the wake of this reign of terror. One came from the NAACP, which, along with the American Council on Race Relations and a wide range of black and white organizations, convened the National Emergency Committee Against Mob Violence. The committee was charged with pressuring President Truman "to throw the full force of the federal government behind our actions and sentiments in bringing before the bar of justice and convicting the lynchers." The group appealed to churches, business associations, and labor unions to fight the battle against mob violence. They also sent a delegation to meet President Truman on September 19, 1946. That meeting resulted in the formation of the President's Committee on Civil Rights. In October of 1947, that committee issued a report titled *To Secure These Rights,* which, among other things, signaled the impact of racial discrimination on the moral standing of the United States around the world. The reality of Cold War politics had begun to shape how black people in the United States acted politically.

The other response came from Paul Robeson. At a rally in Madison Square Garden on September 12, 1946, Robeson directly challenged the Truman administration. He said,

> *This swelling wave of lynch murders and mob assaults against Negro men and women represents the ultimate limit of bestial brutality to which the enemies of democracy, be they German-Nazis or American Ku Kluxers, are ready to go on imposing their will. . . . What about it, President Truman? Why have you failed to speak out against this evil?*

Robeson could not have cared less about America's moral standing around the globe. For him, the idea of the United States as the defender of the free world was a lie. Back home black people languished as second-class citizens subject to arbitrary violence. So, with Du Bois, he called for a massive gathering in Washington, D.C., an American Crusade to End Lynching, "to demand that the killers be prosecuted and the Congress enact a federal antilynching law." More than 3,000 black and white delegates, including Albert Einstein, gathered in Washington on September 23, 1946.

Later that day a delegation, led by Robeson, met with President Truman. The delegates urged the president to act quickly to address the rash of lynchings. Harper Sibley, president of the United Council of Church Women, went as far as to say that the federal government's reluctance on this matter was inconsistent with what the United States had said at the Nuremberg trials. Truman bristled at the suggestion and "reminded" the delegation that Britain and the United States were the "last refuge of freedom in the world." Robeson countered. He considered Britain, with its colonialist policies and the atrocities that these had provoked, to be one of the greatest purveyors of evil in the world. He also told President Truman that black people were willing to defend themselves if need be, warning that "foreign intervention would be in order if mob violence was not stopped." With those words looming between them, President Truman declared the meeting over.

The line in the sand had been drawn. You were either with the United States or its enemy. There was no in between. And the stakes were deadly. Livelihoods would eventually be lost as witch hunts in the name of freedom destroyed people. Robeson would become one of its most famous victims.

Walter White made a choice. He criticized Robeson's efforts, accusing him of confusing "the public mind," and tried to quash any further attempt to link black freedom in the United States to global struggles (a view that defined much of the politics of the previous decades—including his own and that of the NAACP). The United States had to assert its moral leadership in the world, and that required, White claimed, ending racial discrimination at home. The country's oldest civil rights organization now believed that racial justice was a domestic matter—one that meant aligning our practices with national ideals and embracing anti-communism. It drew a line in the sand too.

This was the black liberal compact that set the terms for a new black liberal agenda on civil rights, an agenda in which anti-discrimination policy would free the American Idea to guide the world. In some ways, White and many other black leaders saw the writing on the wall: the Cold War had changed the terrain, and the black radical politics of the 1930s and 1940s was among its many casualties. Criticisms of American foreign policy were increasingly unacceptable, and black politics that rejected the American Idea were off-limits as legitimate forms of dissent. This would define the parameters of black liberalism: anti-communist civil rights, a compact that would limit black politics to domestic issues based in an abiding faith in America as the leader of the free world. White doubled down on America with the hope that, in doing so, black people would become free.

Two weeks after his meeting with President Truman, Paul Robeson was called before the Joint Fact-Finding Committee on Un-American Activities.

2. The Strategy of Deracialization

In 1976, at the Democratic National Convention in New York City, Representative Barbara Jordan of Texas stepped to the podium in Madison Square Garden. The convention would eventually nominate Jimmy Carter and Walter Mondale as the Democratic ticket, but on this day, the power of black women was on full display. Jordan spoke of the challenge facing the Democratic Party and appealed to consensus.

> Are we to be one people bound together by common spirit, sharing in a common endeavor; or will we become a divided nation? For all of its uncertainty, we cannot flee the future. We must not become the "New Puritans" and reject our society. We must address and master the future together. It can be done if we restore the belief that we share a sense of national community, that we share a common endeavor. It can be done.

Of course, this reach for consensus required coming to terms with the issues of racism (and sexism) that convulsed the nation.

What had become painfully clear since the height of the civil rights movement was that large numbers of African Americans continued to suffer chronic unemployment, live in dilapidated housing, and face increased surveillance as calls for law and order became louder and more commonplace. Moreover, America was still reeling from Black Power, urban rebellions, protests over Vietnam, the sexual revolution, the impact of Watergate, and the volatile white backlash that came with increased economic insecurity. Jordan's optimism had to confront the turmoil of the nation and the racial habits that remained deeply rooted despite the successes of the civil rights movement. The question was how?

A second narrowing of black liberal politics began, at least theoretically, in the mid-1970s. The political scientist Charles V. Hamilton, who co-wrote with Stokely Carmichael (Kwame Ture) *Black Power: The Politics of Liberation,* authored a position paper for the national Democratic Party and put forward an answer to Jordan. He argued that, in light of Richard Nixon's victory in 1972 and the white backlash engulfing the nation, the Democratic Party, if it was to have any chance in the 1976 presidential election, had to change the way it engaged race. He advised the party and black political candidates to deemphasize racial matters and to promote universal issues that connected different constituencies. He recommended in 1973, for example, that the issue of full employment applied "to the total society, not only to blacks and other traditionally stigmatized minorities." All who suffered from the economic downturn would support such a measure. This approach, Hamilton proposed, would rob the Republican Party of racial wedge issues aimed at breaking the alliance of "blacks, labor, liberal, [and] white ethnics." For Hamilton, the best way to help black people was to look like you were not trying to help black people.

Of course, the underlying assumption of this view is that those politicians who "deracialized" actually *were* planning to work for progressive policies that would help black communities. Inwardly, they remained committed to racial justice; everyone was just undercover. What this really means, of course, is that the presence of white racism required deracialization in order to elect politicians who would help dismantle racism.

165

But the strategy didn't work, even as African Americans appeared to make political gains. Broader constituencies eventually elected black politicians (for example, Douglass Wilder in Virginia, Carol Moseley Braun in Illinois, David Dinkins in New York City, and Deval Patrick in Massachusetts), but the value gap and racial habits persisted, distorting the political process. Large numbers of white working-class Democrats bolted to Ronald Reagan in 1980. Bill Clinton sought to assure those Reagan Democrats that he was not beholden to the traditional Democratic base as his strategy of triangulation pulled the party more to the center-right of the ideological spectrum. At the very moment the strategy of deracialization took hold among a certain group of black liberals, white anxieties and fears bolstered the value gap with the culture wars, mass incarceration, anti-welfare politics, and the Contract with America. Even "deracialized" elected officials had a hard time navigating the political and cultural climate.

Deracialization became the handcuffs everyone should have seen it as from the start. Many black politicians chose not to speak directly to specific issues confronting their communities without translating those concerns into a more "universal" language that would not trigger white fears. Others who relied on the strategy to get elected had to govern in such a way as not to reveal themselves as *black* politicians.

By the 1990s, as the political scientist Fredrick Harris notes, deracialization had become a strategy for race-neutral black candidates seeking white support, who avoided racial issues like the plague. Candidates had to distance themselves from or denounce black activists deemed too radical by white voters. Any hint of the racial politics of old, like the electoral politics of Black Power, had to be discarded. To gain any power in the first place, politicians had to pretend race wasn't a factor at all.

If the concerns of black communities were to get any traction, it would have to be by way of a form of what Harris calls "wink and nod" politics. Black voters would elect black politicians with the understanding that the politicians are constrained by white racism in terms of what they can address explicitly. But black voters are to trust them implicitly—because they are black, we assume that they will act on behalf of the interests of black people. The danger of this trust is obvious. Black voters can easily find themselves saddled with politicians who symbolically represent them, but who have no intention, out of self-interest, of advocating on their behalf in any specific way. In place of any serious attempt to address racial inequality, we get something hollow, little more than symbols and tidy speeches.

Deracialization reveals two interesting features of black liberalism: (1) the requirement that black leaders represent only the interests of black people to the powers that be (a tenet I associate with traditional black liberals) and (2) the demand that black inclusion in American life depends upon getting beyond race (which I associate with post-black liberals). In this sense, our political options have narrowed to a choice between variants *within* the constraints of black liberalism: debates between traditional black liberals, who embrace racial representation, and post-black liberals, who commend racial transcendence—or some odd hybrid of the two. Either you're black or you're blank.

3. The Jesse Jackson Phenomenon

The Democratic presidential campaigns of Jesse Jackson in 1984 and 1988 greatly accelerated this dynamic. In 1984, Jackson engaged in an insurgent campaign that circumvented the power of black elected officials as representatives of black communities. In some ways, the campaign made explicit the tension between two classes of traditional black liberals within black communities: elected officials and those who led protests.

At the eleventh annual legislative weekend of the Congressional Black Caucus (CBC) in 1981, participants grappled with the nature of black leadership at the dawn of the Reagan era. What would black leadership look like moving forward? Was there a need for a single charismatic leader? The CBC represented the enormous expansion of elected black officials not just in Congress but also around the country. Their presence suggested a shift from a massive mobilization of people in the streets ("movement politics") to a different kind of political arena, where elections and governance mattered. Instead of one leader, members of the CBC were thinking of a model of "communal leadership" made up of people with different skill sets and playing different roles.

Organizations like the NAACP, the Southern Christian Leadership Conference, the National Urban League, and Operation PUSH were seen as relics of the past. Roy Wilkins, the longtime executive director of the NAACP, died and Vernon Jordan stepped down from the leadership of the National Urban League. Matters of black leadership were changing. In response, people like Representative Walter E. Fauntroy, Democratic delegate in the United States House from the District of Columbia and chair of the CBC, said, "We do not have a single leader, nor do the times dictate that there be." Here Fauntroy echoed the sentiments expressed by Roger Wilkins in a *New York Times* editorial on September 28, 1981: "Times are hard and changing. We blacks need to be innovative and sacrificing to meet the old challenges in new forms as well as the truly new challenges, as President Reagan might say. What we don't need is a new, media appointed leader."

Two years later the Joint Center for Political and Economic Studies released a position paper on the "Outlook for a Black Presidential Candidacy." The center maintained that a campaign would, among other things, "encourage black voter registration" and "give prominence to issues of special concern to blacks." Such a candidacy would also potentially "intensify racial polarization of the electorate" and "fragment rather than unify black political leadership."

But a year later, the Reverend Jesse Jackson launched his presidential campaign, and Fauntroy and Wilkins celebrated him as the leader of black America—"the embodiment of collective black aspirations!" They totally reversed themselves.

Jackson inserted himself as *the* leader of black America as he engaged in an effort, however undefined, to revitalize black politics within the confines of the Democratic Party. Louis Farrakhan, the leader of the Nation of Islam, joined the campaign and the Fruit of Islam, the paramilitary wing of the Nation, provided Jackson with security. Here two distinctive traditions joined together, however briefly, to voice a collective black political ambition. Maulana Karenga, a black nationalist and founder of Kwaanza, supported Jackson. He was joined by Reverend Herbert Daughtry of the Black United Front and by the leadership of the National Baptist Convention, an organization of more than 6.5 million black people. Many on the white left also became a part of the campaign, as Jackson's platform included deep cuts in defense spending, a call for a bilateral nuclear freeze, and the redistribution of billions of dollars for job training, public housing, and urban renewal. Here was a political moment, a rainbow coalition, that called together the disparate ideologies within black communities, and it electrified black America.

I remember the 1984 campaign, because I was able to attend the Democratic National Convention in San Francisco as a special guest of the Mississippi delegation. I was only fifteen years old, but I had been active in the politics of my small town. Dorothy Miles, a leader of the Jackson County Democratic Party, thought it would be a great opportunity for me to witness the political process in action. My state representative, Pat Presley, helped me find the support to attend the convention; it was an experience I will never forget. The Mississippi delegation had the best seats of any delegation. I was able to see the late Governor Mario Cuomo deliver his "Tale of Two Cities" speech and sat amazed as Reverend Jackson challenged the nation.

All around me, though, intense battles were raging within the convention. The established black political class had thrown its support behind Walter Mondale. The likes of Charlie Rangel, Julian Bond, Coretta Scott King, and Andrew Young were all in that camp. Jackson had led a small coup. He had circumvented the power of traditional elites—black liberals among them—and appealed directly to black people. Their excitement and energy brought him to the halls of the convention, and like a political maverick, Jackson challenged the status quo and offered a progressive vision for the party and the country. Some three million Americans voted for him. In this sense, he brought the civil rights movement squarely into the electoral process in a way never seen before.

By 1988, though, that vision had morphed into a clear effort to transform the black freedom struggle into the left wing of the Democratic Party. The 1988 campaign had a decidedly different feel from the 1984 campaign. Jackson had more money and a better organization. This wasn't the same grassroots effort as the first campaign. Jackson attracted close to seven million votes and won several primaries. The success of his campaigns helped change the Democratic Party by eliminating winner-take-all primaries and challenging the power of superdelegates. His campaigns also helped elect black politicians, as the voter registration campaigns brought black voters to the polls. Sadly, though, much of this didn't translate into substantive improvement in the everyday lives of black people. Instead, Jackson and his cronies asserted their individual influence within the party. In 1989, Jackson's campaign manager, Ron Brown, was elected the chairman of the Democratic National Committee and in 1992 he played a key role in the election of Bill Clinton. Ironically, Brown would help develop the Clinton strategy to contain the African American base and move the Democratic Party to the right and firmly into the hands of big money. All of this set the stage for the election of Barack Obama in 2008.

In fact, candidate Obama took a page right out of Jackson's play-book. Most of the black political elites had thrown their support behind Hillary Clinton. But Obama took his campaign directly to the people. After the victory in Iowa, black politicians and civil rights leaders—the traditional black liberals—had to either join him or risk marginalization. Jackson may have taken umbrage. On Fox News, he whispered off-camera that Obama should "have his nuts cut off" for talking down to black people. Jackson has been marginal ever since. But no matter his current status as a political outsider, both of his presidential campaigns helped secure the triumph of the black liberal compact by braiding together the black struggle for freedom and the Democratic Party.

Jackson figured himself as the successor to Dr. King and, in doing so, he narrowed our understanding of the black freedom struggle. Here the grassroots organizing and the array of political organizations that made up that fight were reduced to a bland black liberal politics with a charismatic preacher as its head. It was a tidy, if not entirely inaccurate, story: one that moves seamlessly from Dr. King to Reverend Jackson to President Obama.

These three historical moments—the black liberal compact of 1946, the strategy of deracialization of 1976, and the Jesse Jackson campaigns of 1984 and 1988—illustrate how black liberalism became the dominant, if not the only, political game in town. The triumph of black liberalism happened even as the material conditions of black life deteriorated and as the institutional life of black America collapsed. In other words, traditional and now post-black liberals have been on watch in all phases of black life—as elected representatives in statehouses and in Congress, as mayors, as protest leaders, as members of long-standing civil rights organizations, and now as president—at the very moment black America is suffering a slow and agonizing death. We should free our political imaginations from their stranglehold.

RACIAL ADVOCACY GAME

Conservative black liberals couldn't agree more. For them, traditional and post-black liberals have sold black people down the river. People like Shelby Steele, Jason L. Riley, and Ben Carson believe that black liberal leaders often benefit personally by peddling government dependence and repeatedly claiming victimization. Black people would do better, Riley suggests, if liberals would "stop helping us" and black people took responsibility for the "culture of failure" that dominates black communities.

Juan Williams, a political analyst for Fox News, believes that much of the misery engulfing black communities resulted not only from bad behavior but also because of bad black leadership, what he calls "the leadership gap." Conservative black liberals like Williams believe black leaders have sent the wrong message to poor black people: that instead of emphasizing the importance of strong families, education, and hard work, African American leaders are fixated on racism and engaged in a "tired rant . . . about what people didn't do and what white people should do. This rant puts black people in the role of hapless victims waiting for one thing—white guilt to bail them out." For Shelby Steele, this sense of guilt and shame has led liberal America to repent through "a moral manipulation that exaggerates inequality and unfairness in American life in order to justify overreaching public policies and programs." Black liberal leaders benefit as the brokers of that guilt and shame.

Conservatives are onto something here. I agree with their frustration with black leadership, but for dramatically different reasons. What they rightly single out is something I want to call *the racial advocacy game,* the way some people parlay politics into a whole lot of money and gain a lot of influence for themselves advocating for black people but do little for black democratic life.

On February 18, 2014, a group of black leaders held a 90-minute meeting with President Obama. A lot had happened since Obama's election. The Great Black Depression continued to ravage black communities. Conservatives in several states fought to pass voter ID laws that threatened to disenfranchise black voters. And Trayvon Martin's death had triggered the conscience of young black people throughout the country. Marc Morial of the National Urban League; Reverend Al Sharpton of the National Action Network; Wade Henderson of the Leadership Conference on Civil and Human Rights; Lorraine Miller, the interim president and CEO of the NAACP; Patricia Rosier of the National Bar Association; Melanie Campbell of the National Coalition on Black Civic Participation; and Sherrilyn Ifill of the NAACP Legal Defense and Educational Fund were among those who attended the meeting. These were the big guns of the civil rights establishment. The topics ranged from voter suppression to income inequality and jobs to state laws that "threatened civil rights such as 'stand your ground.'" During the meeting Morial presented the president with a document called "The 21st Century Agenda for Jobs and Freedom." Morial and Sharpton reported that the meeting was substantive and that the president's plans were aligned, for the most part, with the agenda of the group.

I was struck by the meeting—not so much by its content, but because it seemed so familiar. Almost exactly four years earlier, on February 10, 2010, Morial, Sharpton, and the then-president of the NAACP,

Ben Jealous, had held a press conference on a snowy day in Washington, D.C., to report about a different (but decidedly similar) meeting with President Obama. Obama had convened what some dubbed an "urban economy summit" in the Oval Office. Black liberal leaders pushed to alleviate black unemployment, which at the time hovered around 15 percent. They wanted a stronger focus on communities with high unemployment, and they wanted $150 billion of the Troubled Asset Relief Program (TARP) funds "to be redirected to state and local governments to hire workers to provide critical services in underserved communities."

A lot has happened since 2010. One thing that hasn't happened, however, is a full accounting of what actually resulted from that meeting. No one reported whether or not the TARP funds made their way to state and local governments for the purposes outlined. As for black unemployment—well, President Obama has consistently put forward the position that improving the economy generally will disproportionately benefit the communities most hit. The only thing we know for sure is that this has not been the case. Our "fearless" black leaders seem to have accomplished nothing when it comes to ameliorating the effects of the Great Black Depression.

Fast-forward to the aftermath of the meeting in 2014: many of the same so-called black leaders reported that their agenda was in alignment with the president's, and offered little beyond the theatrics of racial representation—a press conference and black liberal bromides aimed at securing their place as spokespeople for all black folk. What does it suggest that their agenda aligns with the president's plan? What have been the president's plans for black America over the course of his presidency? Only the so-called black leaders know.

Some might cry that what has transpired between 2010 and 2014 has little to do with the failure of black leaders to hold President Obama accountable for black social misery or with black liberal theatrics. The real problem has been and continues to be Republican obstructionism. The argument implies that if it were not for the shenanigans of the right wing, President Obama and black leaders would have substantively addressed the crisis engulfing black America. But this claim is a red herring. I am not denying that Republicans have stood in the way of much of the president's agenda. The issue isn't President Obama and his policies or his failures. The real issue is the implication of this form of black leadership.

The idea that you can have black leaders representing the interests of all black people but who are not accountable to black constituents kills black democratic life. Black people end up outsourcing their democratic responsibilities to people deemed caretakers of their interests and stewards of their futures. The different interests within black communities get ignored. Black people are reduced to an undifferentiated mass in need of representation by a particular black political class, whether elected or self-appointed.

This approach obscures the need for critical debate and reflection among black people. It also undermines mechanisms of accountability as black elites broker on behalf of black people whose interests are, so it is claimed, readily identifiable. This approach was clearly evident in the February 2014 meeting with Obama. These weren't elected officials accountable to voters. They were traditional black liberals talking with a post-black liberal about what mattered to black America. With them around, we don't have to engage in politics. These folks will do it for us, or we will do it with them at the front of another damn march. We simply need to turn out and vote every two years for a Democrat. No wonder conservative black liberals are so upset.

All of this grows out of white supremacy: the idea that black folk need someone or some organization to represent them to white people, and the demand for a black spokesperson becomes *the* form of black political leadership. We need our Moses, our messiah. Here the charismatic leader, accountable to no one, ends up reproducing the very practice and habits that disfigured black democratic life in the first place.

I am not suggesting that all forms of black politics end up doing this. But black liberalism does it. This form of politics, with traditional black liberals like the Reverends Sharpton and Jackson, and post-black liberals like President Obama, with their "winks and nods," combines with a bad story of black democratic struggle. It's a story that glorifies a particular version of Martin Luther King and draws a straight line between his struggles and President Obama. It makes us all patriots and strangles our political imaginations by radically limiting the range of black political action. The whole business of black politics becomes the political project of black liberals, with their latent desire for the disappearance of black America. Looks like we have been accomplices in our own demise after all.

CHAPTER EIGHT

A REVOLUTION OF VALUE

I n response to the grand juries' non-indictments in the Eric Garner and Michael Brown cases, the Reverend Al Sharpton and other civil rights leaders organized what they called the Justice for All march on Washington. They wanted the federal government to ensure the police officers involved in the deadly shootings would be prosecuted. Sharpton likened the march to the 1963 March on Washington, which helped push through Congress the Civil Rights Act of 1964. "It's time for a national march to deal with a national crisis," Sharpton declared. "How many people have to die before people understand this is not an illusion? This is a reality that America has got to come to terms with."

On December 13, 2014, thousands of people joined Sharpton and the families of Eric Garner, Michael Brown, Trayvon Martin, Tamir Rice, Akai Gurley, John Crawford III, and Amadou Diallo (all of whom died at the hands of the police). People chanted, "Black lives matter"; "I can't breathe," echoing the last words of Garner; and "Hands up, don't shoot," referring to the senseless death of Michael Brown in Ferguson, as they marched on the Capitol. It was familiar and tragic racial theater.

Speakers were set for the program (including civil rights leaders, members of the families, and, of course, Sharpton himself), but young organizers abruptly walked onstage and demanded to be heard. They came to the march to protest police violence and racism, and saw instead a VIP section, which confirmed for them that this was just a showcase for a "celebrity activist" who wanted to hijack a youth-led movement. Young people around the stage shouted, "Let them speak. . . . If we don't get it, shut it down." Erika Totten from Alexandria, Virginia, grabbed the microphone and said, "We have been out in Ferguson and D.C. and New York, and we started this uprising." Johnetta Elzie, a protester from Ferguson, recounted the then-127-day-long struggle in her city, and how she had been shot by rubber bullets and tear-gassed nine times. "This movement was started by the young people. We started this. There should be young people all over this stage."

A series of protests around the Washington, D.C., metropolitan area later that day showcased the differences between what Sharpton and the traditional black leaders were doing and what a burgeoning new movement aspired to do. DC Ferguson, a group of young activists in the DC metro area who hoped to connect what happened in Ferguson to the broader issue of police violence in the country, engaged in direct actions that blocked traffic on a key highway and disrupted business as usual throughout the city. No one, they argued, should be comfortable until racial justice is a reality. For them, Sharpton and his ilk stood in the way of fundamental change. They were part of the problem.

This wasn't the first time young activists questioned Sharpton's role and commitment to their efforts to combat police violence. After a meeting with President Obama on December 2, 2014, Ashley Yates, a Ferguson protester and cofounder of Millennial Activists United (MAU), tweeted:

> We sat around this table and listened to @theRevAl
> as he spoke of the work WE put in. He didn't know a
> single one of our names.

He never set foot on a protest site. Never attended
any actions planned by local organizers, but then got
up there and tried to praise.

He walked his black ass clean out of the room without
so much as an INTRODUCTION to any of us. Not a
single word.

We know what this movement is about: People Power.
And what it's not about: Late Negroes in suits tryna
cling to glory days @theRevAl.

Sharpton dismissed the criticisms. He told the crowd in D.C. not to let
"provocateurs" and issues of "generations and race" divide them.

For Sharpton, these were unorganized young people seeking the
limelight—a limelight he commanded. He intimated as much during his eulogy for Michael Brown: "Some leaders mad about other
leaders. . . . More folk worried about getting on the program than de-
veloping a program." Now he refused to pull any punches. In a *Washington Post* profile, Sharpton was brazen in his disregard for the young
activists. "I hear them saying that [w]e don't want Sharpton taking
over our movement. But my question is, what movement? Y'all ain't
got nothing to take over," he declared. Sharpton went on to say, talking about himself in the third person, "How come Sharpton's leading
the march? Cause I organized the march. I brought the crowd. I got
the permit. Those Porta-Potties cost us $20,000. You want to run the
march. Fine. Get your own damn Porta-Potties." In the end, Sharpton felt no need to account for his approach to activism or his place
in front of the cameras. As he put it, "If I didn't exist, they'd have to
invent me."

Something deeper is going on here than a generational split. The young activists who challenged Sharpton questioned the very model of leadership he represents. For them, the idea of a single male voice that stands in for the interests of all black people is a dead option. Even one of Sharpton's youth leaders acknowledged the problem: "The issue with my generation is we're more the Occupy organizing model. You know, everyone can be a leader, that kind of thing." Sharpton bristles at such an idea. He has been working hard for most of his adult life to be the "Head Negro in Charge" (HNIC). A democratic model of leadership does not jibe with that aspiration. But, in one sense, Sharpton is right. The way race works in this country, if black people refused the idea of an HNIC, someone, somewhere would invent one and force him down our throats.

In the end, the bankruptcy of black liberalism and its model of leadership, along with the collapse of black institutional life, make the current crisis in black America all the more dangerous. Sharpton, whom I consider a friend, is just one symptom. The problem of black leadership is all the more troublesome given that we no longer have an abundance of safe and creative spaces to combat racism, and the dominant form of black politics of the past half century has proved ineffective in tackling racial injustice today. Black America has never faced anything like this before. And leaders like the Reverend Sharpton aren't saying a mumbling word. Something has to change.

If we are committed to American democracy, and by some twisted fate I must be, we have to work for something more transformative. *A revolution of value* upends the belief that white people are more valued than others. And that goes beyond a mere statement of our commitment to racial equality. We have to break the racial habits that give life to the value gap, and that starts with changes in our social and political arrangements. Most habits come to us in the context of our living in so-cial worlds not of our own making—in our neighborhoods and broader communities. Without question, habits move us about until something gets in the way and interrupts the usual order of things. When they are no longer taken for granted, habits can change, because we notice they are out of sync with the task before us, with the moment we live in, or with the person we hope to be.

In my more hopeful moments, I believe that the little boy who played Tonka trucks with me in Moss Point—now old enough to have his own son or daughter—doesn't think of black children as niggers like his father did. Times have changed, and the blatant signs of white su-premacy have been dismantled. But I am less optimistic about whether he believes that poor black children need a social safety net or decent schools or that those children's parents deserve an equal opportunity to earn a living wage and to own a home without a subprime loan. Or that they deserve to grow up in neighborhoods where they aren't always under suspicion or under surveillance, where jails or prisons or prema-ture death do not cut short any reason for them to dream. Given that, I suppose I still believe he thinks, like his dad, that I am a nigger. For what else does the word mean? It is just shorthand for a life less valued.

Remaking American democracy is going to require a revolution of value to transform our habits. This isn't a call, as President Obama made during the press conference after the George Zimmerman trial, "to widen the circle of compassion and understanding in our communi-ties." Something more expansive has to happen. It has to occur at many levels: in government, in communities, among individuals. Besides, calls to "widen circles of compassion and understanding" only reinforce the belief that durable racial inequality is, at its root, a problem of racial rec-onciliation: that if we could all just get along, our racial problems would disappear. This is one dimension of the illusion that protects American innocence. "Getting along" does not measure up to a more fundamental concern about racial justice or get at how we are *all* complicit in racial injustice. The illusion hides the rot.

A revolution of value would seek to uproot those ways of seeing and living that allow Americans to support racial equality and yet live in ways that suggest they believe otherwise. It is a revolution to close, once and for all, the value gap—to finally rid the country of niggers. It involves three basic components: (1) a change in how we view government; (2) a change in how we view black people; and (3) a change in how we view what ultimately matters to us as Americans.

These shifts are not abstract considerations. They get to the marrow of what blocks the way to real change in this country, and they will require political mobilization and massive disruption of the status quo.

Since the death of Trayvon Martin, young people have been doing just that. They have engaged in direct actions in which they have stopped traffic, held sit-ins in state capitols, staged die-ins in places of business, interrupted brunch among the 1 percent in New York, and directly challenged the police from Ferguson to Oakland. Even during President Obama's speech on the fiftieth anniversary of Selma, young protesters interrupted him with drums and chants: "Ferguson is here." "We want change." And "This is what democracy looks like." Alongside these young people are other Americans, like those in the Forward Together movement in North Carolina and people who are organizing with fast-food workers and Walmart employees for a livable wage, doing the hard work of democracy. They are in the streets, in voting booths, in courtrooms, and in their communities, block by block, callused hand by callused hand, facing the doubters, challenging our view of government and of black people, and laying the foundation for a true revolution of value. These activists force us, whether we agree with them or not, to think about how we currently live our lives. In short, they shed light on our racial habits and create the conditions, however fleeting, for us to change them.

Change How We View Government

For more than three decades, we have been bludgeoned with an idea of government that has little to no concern for the public good. Big government is bad, we are told. It is inefficient, and its bloated bureaucracies are prone to corruption. Even Democrats, especially since Bill Clinton, have taken up this view. For example, Obama says, "We don't need big government; we need smart government."

For some on the right, big government is bad because it aims to redistribute wealth to those who are lazy and undeserving. "Big government" is just a shorthand for dreaded entitlement programs—all too often coded language for race. In this view, "big government" is the primary agent of enforcing racial equality, taking hard-earned stuff from white Americans and giving it to undeserving others. Government cannot do such a thing, they argue, without infringing on the rights of white Americans. And even government-mandated redistribution will not solve the problem. As Barry Goldwater put the point in 1964, "No matter how we try, we cannot pass a law that will make you like me or me like you. The key to racial and religious tolerance lies not in laws alone but, ultimately, in the hearts of men." From this perspective, government plays no role in changing our racial habits. Why would we want to make it bigger?

But Goldwater failed to realize that governmental indifference can harden hearts, and government action can create conditions that soften them. People's attitudes aren't static or untouchable. They are molded by the quality of interactions with others, and one of the great powers of government involves shaping those interactions—not determining them in any concrete sense, but defining the parameters within which people come to know each other and live together. Today, for example, most Americans don't believe women should be confined to the home raising children, or subjected to crude advances and sexist remarks by men. The women's-rights movement put pressure on the government, which in turn passed laws that helped change some of our beliefs about women. Similarly, the relative progress of the 1960s did not happen merely by using the blunt instruments of the law. Change emerged from the ways those laws, with grassroots pressure, created new patterns of interactions, and ultimately new habits. Neither Obama's election to the presidency nor my appointment as a Princeton professor would have happened were it not for these new patterns and habits.

None of this happens overnight. It takes time and increasing vigilance to protect and secure change. I was talking with a close friend and he mentioned a basic fact: that we were only fifteen years removed from the passage of the Voting Rights Act of 1965 when Ronald Reagan was elected president and Republicans began to dismantle the gains of the black freedom struggle. Civil rights legislation and the policies of the Great Society had just started to reshape our interactions when they started to be rolled back. We barely had a chance to imagine America anew—to pursue what full employment might look like, to let the abolition of the death penalty settle in, to question seriously the morality of putting people in prison cells, and to enact policies that would undo what the 1968 Kerner Commission described as "two Americas"— before the attack on "big government" or, more precisely, the attack on racial equality was launched. The objective was to shrink the size of government ("to starve the beast") and to limit its domestic responsibilities to ensuring economic efficiency and national defense. Democrats eventually buckled, and this is the view of government, no matter who is in office, that we have today. It has become a kind of touchstone of faith among most Americans that government is wasteful and should be limited in its role—that it shouldn't intrude on our lives. Politicians aren't the only ones who hold this view. Many Americans do, too. Now we can't even imagine serious talk of things like full employment or the abolition of prisons.

We have to change our view of government, especially when it comes to racial matters. Government policy ensured the vote for African Americans and dismantled legal segregation. Policy established a social safety net for the poor and elderly; it put in place the conditions for the growth of our cities. All of this didn't happen simply because of individual will or thanks to some abstract idea of America. It was tied up with our demands and expectations. Goldwater was wrong. So was Reagan. And, in many ways, so is Obama. Our racial habits are shaped by the kind of society in which we live, and our government plays a big role in shaping that society. As young children, our community offers us a way of seeing the world; it lets us know what is valuable and sacred, and what stands as virtuous behavior and what does not. When Michael Brown's body was left in the street for more than four hours, it sent a clear message about the value of black lives. When everything in our society says that we should be less concerned about black folk, that *they* are dangerous, that no specific policies can address their misery, we say to our children and to everyone else that these people are "less than"—that they fall outside of our moral concern. We say, without using the word, that they are niggers.

One way to change that view is to enact policies that suggest otherwise. Or, to put it another way, to change our view of government, we must change our demands of government. For example, for the past fifty years African American unemployment has been twice that of white unemployment. The 2013 unemployment rate for African Americans stood at 13.1 percent, the highest annual black unemployment rate in more than seventy years. Social scientists do not generally agree on the causes of this trend. Some attribute it to the fact that African Americans are typically the "last hired and first fired." Others point to changes in the nature of the economy; still others point to overt racial discrimination in the labor market. No matter how we account for the numbers, the fact remains that most Americans see double-digit black unemployment as "normal." However, a large-scale, comprehensive jobs agenda with a living wage designed to put Americans, and explicitly African Americans, to work would go a long way toward uprooting the racial habits that inform such a view. It would counter the nonsense that currently stands as a reason for long-term black unemployment in public debate: black folk are lazy and don't want to work.

If we hold the view that government plays a crucial role in ensuring the public good—if we believe that all Americans, no matter their race or class, can be vital contributors to our beloved community—then we reject the idea that some populations are disposable, that some people can languish in the shadows while the rest of us dance in the light. The question "Am I my brother's or my sister's keeper?" is not just a question for the individual or a mantra to motivate the private sector. It is a question answered in the social arrangements that aim to secure the goods and values we most cherish as a community. In other words, we need an idea of government that reflects the value of *all* Americans, not just white Americans or a few people with a lot of money.

We need government seriously committed to racial justice. As a nation, we can never pat ourselves on the back about racial matters. We have too much blood on our hands. Remembering that fact—our inheritance, as Wendell Berry said—does not amount to beating ourselves over the head, or wallowing in guilt, or trading in race cards. Remembering our national sins serves as a check and balance against national hubris. We're reminded of what we are capable of, and our eyes are trained to see that ugliness when it rears its head. But when we disremember—when we forget about the horrors of lynching, lose sight of how African Americans were locked into a dual labor market because of explicit racism, or ignore how we exported our racism around the world—we free ourselves from any sense of accountability. Concern for others and a sense of responsibility for the whole no longer matter. Cruelty and indifference become our calling cards.

We have to isolate those areas in which long-standing trends of racial inequality short-circuit the life chances of African Americans. In addition to a jobs agenda, we need a comprehensive government response to the problems of public education and mass incarceration. And I do mean a *government* response. Private interests have overrun both areas, as privatization drives school reform (and the education of our children is lost in the boisterous battles between teachers' unions and private interests) and as big business makes enormous profits from the warehousing of black and brown people in prisons. Let's be clear: private interests or market-based strategies will not solve the problems we face as a country or bring about the kind of society we need. We have to push for massive government investment in early childhood education and in shifting the center of gravity of our society from punishment to restorative justice. We can begin to enact the latter reform by putting an end to the practice of jailing children. Full stop. We didn't jail children in the past. We don't need to now.

In sum, government can help us go a long way toward uprooting racial habits with policies that support jobs with a living wage, which would help wipe out the historic double-digit gap between white and black unemployment; take an expansive approach to early childhood education, which social science research consistently says profoundly affects the life chances of black children; and dismantle the prison-industrial complex. We can no longer believe that disproportionately locking up black men and women constitutes an answer to social ills.

This view of government cannot be dismissed as a naïve pipe dream, because political considerations relentlessly attack our political imaginations and limit us to the status quo. We are told before we even open our mouths that this particular view won't work or that it will never see the light of day. We've heard enough of that around single-payer health care reform and other progressive policies over the Obama years. Such defeatist attitudes conspire to limit our imaginations and make sure that the world stays as it is. But those of us who don't give a damn about the rules of the current political game must courageously organize, advocate, and insist on the moral and political significance of a more robust role for government. We have to change the terms of political debate.

Something dramatic has to happen. American democracy has to be remade. John Dewey, the American philosopher, understood this:

> *The very idea of democracy, the meaning of democracy, must be continually explored afresh; it has to be constantly discovered and rediscovered, remade and reorganized; while the political and economic and social institutions in which it is embodied have to be remade and reorganized to meet the changes that are going on in the development of new needs on the part of human beings and new resources for satisfying these needs.*

Dewey saw American democracy as an unfinished project. He knew that the aims and purposes of this country were not fixed forever in the founding documents, but the particular challenges of our moment required imaginative leaps on behalf of democracy itself. Otherwise, undemocratic forces might prevail; tyranny in the form of the almighty dollar and the relentless pursuit of it might overtake any commitment to the idea of the public good; and bad habits might diminish our moral imaginations.

The remaking of America will not happen inside the Beltway. Too many there have too much invested in the status quo. A more robust idea of government will not emerge from the current political parties. Both are beholden to big money. Substantive change will have to come from us. Or, as the great civil rights leader Ella Baker said, "we are the leaders we've been looking for"—a model of leadership that scares the hell out of the Reverend Sharpton. We will have to challenge the status quo in the streets and at the ballot box. In short, it will take a full-blown democratic awakening to enact this revolution.

On February 7, 2014, I flew to Raleigh, North Carolina, to join with tens of thousands of other like-minded people to protest the draconian laws passed by the North Carolina state legislature. Since 2010, while many people—especially black people—were still reeling from the 2008 recession/depression, Republicans eliminated Medicaid coverage for half a million North Carolinians, passed a voter-ID law designed to disenfranchise primarily African American voters, transferred $90 million from public schools to voucher schools and cut pre-K for 30,000 children, passed a law requiring women about to have an abortion to listen to the heartbeat of the fetus, repealed the earned income tax credit for 900,000 people, and constitutionally banned gay marriage. North Carolina Republicans had declared war. They represented clear examples of those who hold a view of government that hardens hearts and reinforces racial habits.

I watched from afar as the Forward Together moral movement took shape in response. People from all across North Carolina organized and mobilized to take back the state from extremists. The state NAACP, with its charismatic leader, Reverend William Barber II, built a movement from the ground up to challenge what they took to be an all-out assault on the moral and social fabric of the state. The movement was not simply a reaction to Tea Party Republicans. "We started this when the Democrats were in power," Barber said. "We put out the word. The state had not complied with the *Leandro* decision [a 1994 public-education-equity lawsuit]. We still had not given public employees collective bargaining rights. We didn't have a racial justice act." But the actions of the North Carolina GOP intensified the group's efforts. More than 900 people who engaged in nonviolent civil disobedience to protest the Republican agenda were arrested during the 2013 legislative session.

Reverend Barber put out a call across the country for a massive march in February to launch the 2014 Forward Together campaign. Eighty thousand to 100,000 people answered. It was the largest mass demonstration in the South since the Selma march in 1965.

I arrived early. It was cold, and clouds blocked the sun as organizers began to set up. A few people worked on their signs. One sign read PROTECT ALL N.C. CITIZENS with different examples of vulnerable groups written underneath (the mentally ill, the unemployed, teachers, the elderly, students, prisoners, the uninsured, minorities). I was struck from the beginning by the cross-section of people there. Old and young, straight and gay, black, white, and Latino all began to gather.

I asked a few of them why they were marching. Leslie Boyd, a white woman from Asheville, North Carolina, told me about her son, Michael Danforth. He had suffered from a birth defect that made it next to impossible for him to get health insurance. He died in the hospital, and ever since, she has dedicated her life to health care activism. She started a small nonprofit called Western North Carolina Health Advocates, through which she met Reverend Barber. He asked her to join the movement.

The cold weather drove me into the nearby McDonald's, where several people sipped coffee while they waited for the march to begin. I struck up a conversation with Martin Marshall from Atlanta, Georgia, and Ron Gray from Rock Hill, South Carolina. Martin told me a story about his childhood experiences with racism, about the wall that divided his white community from the black community, and how racism was still alive today. "Voter restrictions and access to health care" were the reasons he was marching. Ron was less talkative. He said, "I will give you the short form: injustice. I am here because it is the right place to be."

Sitting next to Martin and Ron was an older white couple, Bill and Betsy Crittendon from Chapel Hill, North Carolina. They were members of an interracial choir called the United Voices of Praise. They had been involved in interracial social issues for a number of years and found the "regressive policies that have come about in this state [to be] just awful, absolutely awful. They have completely reversed the course of this state." Mrs. Crittendon wasn't too optimistic that the march would change the minds of state legislators, but she and her husband understood the long-term significance of the march and the Forward Together movement. "People need to see and hear what this is all about. . . . Every step along the way is a building step [to clear] the way for justice issues."

These were people from different walks of life who understood the common ground of suffering in this country. For them, that understanding did not require anyone to leave the particulars of their suffering at the door. Anti-racism remained a part of their advocacy whether they struggled for universal health care or a living wage. They joined with others to urge a fundamental change in North Carolina and the country that could help break down racial habits. Reverend Barber thinks of their efforts in this way:

> [It's] about showing people the intersectionality of their lives; the intersectionality of their moving together. . . . We have a phrase: we is the most important word in the justice vocabulary. The issue is not what I can do, but what we can do when we stand together, fight together, pray together, and work together, and we feel movement together. (Emphasis added.)

As I finished the conversations in McDonald's, I looked outside. Busload after busload of people had begun to arrive. Before the march began, speakers rallied the crowd. The topics were wide-ranging, from LGBT concerns, the state of public education, issues of immigration and the status of undocumented workers, to racist voter-ID laws. It was an in-the-flesh performance of a multiracial, multi-issue coalition. And whenever someone shouted, "Forward together," the crowd replied, "Not one step back."

Initially, to an outsider looking in, the moment resembled the traditional theater of contemporary American protest. A march serves as a moment of catharsis. People gather, tensions are released, folks go back to business as usual, and the men (and it is typically always men) who lead the march leverage the spotlight for personal gain. But a brief glance beneath the surface of this particular gathering revealed something much more expansive. The march was just the tip of an organizing iceberg. Reverend Barber declared, "The Moral March inaugurates a fresh year of grassroots empowerment, voter education, litigation, and nonviolent direct action."

In other words, this march wasn't a culmination but a catalyst: it dramatized an organizing effort (which preceded the gathering) that encompassed the courtroom, the ballot box, and the streets. For Barber, the work of democracy doesn't happen through marches or backroom deals but through concerted efforts "to change the context in which power operates." Of course, voting matters. But democracy is about the commitment to get one's hands dirty, and that work is often selfless and thankless.

At the heart of those efforts is a more robust conception of government—a belief that government has the capacity to transform lives through focused legislation—and an insistence that we shift the center of moral gravity in North Carolina and in the nation. Five demands guide this insistence: (1) secure pro-labor, anti-poverty policies that ensure economic sustainability; (2) provide well-funded, quality public education to all; (3) stand up for the health of every North Carolinian by promoting health care access and environmental justice across all the state's communities; (4) address the continuing inequalities in the criminal justice system and ensure equality under the law for every person, regardless of race, class, creed, documentation, or sexual preference; and (5) protect and expand voting rights for people of color, immigrants, the elderly, and students to safeguard fair democratic representation. Each demand carries with it an expectation of the role of government in safeguarding the public good and an affirmation of the dignity and standing of all Americans. If we were to embrace these demands as policy, we would be well on our way to a revolution of value.

As we marched from historic Shaw University, the place where the Student Non-Violent Coordinating Committee was founded in April 1960, to the state capitol, Americans from all walks of life expressed a radically egalitarian vision of this country. This vision did not require African Americans to leave their experiences at the door. Alongside demands for marriage equality, cries for support of public education, and calls for a more robust commitment to labor, marchers embraced the call for an anti-racist politics. As Reverend Barber said, "Some people wanted us to emphasize poverty instead of race. But you have to speak the truth. [Race] can be the Achilles' heel of the movement or lend itself to your moral positioning." We have to confront white supremacy, or what Barber calls "the corruption of the spirit and the conscience," as a fundamental contradiction of American democracy, or face the consequences of our silence.

As the march concluded, I stood amazed at the power of ordinary people. Thousands of people had come together, for a moment, to declare their commitment to a radical vision of democracy. This is what has been missing in contemporary American politics. Reverend Barber's inspiring remarks struck a chord that reached back to the nineteenth-century abolitionists, black and white, who decided to become traitors in the name of American democracy. They turned their backs on the slave regime. Barber called us to do the same with the political extremists of our times.

We need the kind of language that's not left or right or conservative or liberal, but moral, fusion language that says look: it's extreme and immoral to suppress the right to vote. It's extreme and immoral to deny Medicaid for millions of poor people. . . . It's extreme and immoral to raise taxes on the working poor by cutting earned income taxes and to raise taxes on the poor and middle class in order to cut taxes for the wealthy. It's extreme and immoral to use power to cut off poor people's water in Detroit. That's immoral! What we need to cut off is that kind of abusive power! It's extreme and immoral to resegregate our schools and underfund our public schools. It's extreme and immoral for people who came from immigrants to now have a mean amnesia and cry out against immigrants and the rights of children. . . . That's not just bad policy, it's against the common good and a disregard for human rights. It's a refusal to lean toward the angels of our better selves. . . . In policy and politics in America, we face two choices. One is the low road to political destruction, and the other is the pathway to higher ground.

Barber finished speaking—preaching, really. The crowd joined hands to sing "We Shall Overcome." The voices were full of emotion and faith, not the sound of trepidation heard in the voices of those who sang the song after Reagan's speech in the Rose Garden. For much of the march, the day had been cloudy and cold. But as he spoke, the sun finally broke through. "The sun has come out," Reverend Barber started to shout. "The sun has come out. We are on our way to higher ground. Even the universe blesses this day. Even the universe says yes to justice, yes to equality, yes to higher ground." Marchers shouted. In front of me stood a white Episcopalian preacher in tears. I wiped my own eyes.

This is the kind of social movement that will transform our idea of government. It insists on the dignity and standing of black people and other marginalized groups, and it argues for a dramatic change in what we as Americans care most about. To be sure, the Forward Together moral movement isn't the only form of struggle we need. (In some ways, Reverend Barber represents the long-standing tradition of the charismatic preacher as leader, although he happens to be aware of the pitfalls of the model of leadership even as he exemplifies it.) It represents just one example of what a democratic awakening must do if we are to change the terms of political debate in this country: it must enact a different way of thinking about government and its relation to the most vulnerable among us.

CHANGE HOW WE VIEW BLACK PEOPLE

Changing the terms of political debate also involves transforming how we "see" black people in America. Most Americans, conservative and liberal, see African Americans as failing. That perception shapes our habits, and our habits, in turn, shape the perception. Black people fail in schools and in the workplace, and we fail our families and our children. Not even the black middle class is safe from these judgments. Aside from obvious exceptions like Kenneth Chenault or Oprah Winfrey, the prevailing stereotype holds that the majority of African Americans are failures. We exhibit bad habits because of a culture of poverty, we are too dependent on government instead of being self-reliant, and we are unwilling to hold ourselves responsible for our own failures. We are perennial victims.

This is a standard position on the right. On the radio show *Bill Bennett's Morning in America* in March 2014, Paul Ryan said as much when he talked about the culture of black unemployment. "We have got this tailspin of culture, in our inner cities in particular, of men not working and just generations of men not even thinking about working or learning the value and the culture of work, and so there is a real culture

197

problem here that has to be dealt with." Ryan's use of *inner city* worked as a racial dog whistle aimed at triggering ideas of lazy black people.

Some liberals have their version of black pathology, too. If conservatives see black people as failures, too often liberals see them as statistical data. Such a view often leads to an approach to black communities as "projects" that renders the actual people who live there invisible. KIPP schools, a public charter school network in underserved communities, come to mind. Black children are vigorously regimented in these schools. Orderliness and obedience are seen as a precondition for instruction. An underlying assumption of this organization is that our children lack discipline and require a strict environment to learn.

A colleague of mine once visited a museum in Philadelphia and noticed three different classes of young children. One was from a Quaker school, and the children laughed and ran, shouting and expressing themselves. Another was from a predominantly white suburban school. The children talked and laughed as they moved about the museum. The other was from a black charter school. The children stood in line with military precision and were repeatedly reprimanded for talking. The teachers, of course, meant well, but the differences in treatment, in expectations, in freedom, were startling.

Both conservatives and liberals rely on assumptions about black people. Conservatives tend to think of black people as responsible for their own failures. Liberals tend to point to environments that make them fail. In both instances, the constant refrain is that black people fail. What gets lost in all this are the actual lives of real black people.

Unfortunately we learn early on the categories to which we are consigned. They work like cages, trapping us in images and assumptions about our capacities as we, perhaps like those black children in the museum, watch others extend their wings and fly. The categories are numerous: thugs, welfare queens, the underclass, absent fathers, criminals, affirmative action babies, lazy, irresponsible, unteachable, etc. It is one of the terrible ironies that this country so efficiently convinces us to occupy that place as our own—even when everything about the category says we are "less than." In the end, black humanity gets squeezed between claims about our failures and concerns over our deficiencies. Lost between both is the fullness of who we are.

The view of African Americans as culturally deficient or broken or as examples of moral failure obscures the real barriers confronting black communities. The truth is this: much of the hell black people catch in this country today is rooted in the enduring legacy of racist practices in every domain of American life—legacies that we ritually deny or acknowledge only in stories about "perfecting the Union." But if we're honest, we see the pervasive effects of those practices in education, in housing, in the labor market, in disparities in health, and in the rate of poverty. In each instance, the practices and habits of white supremacy—practices that shaped the lives of my parents—ensured that white people would benefit and black people would struggle. And, again, we only tried to undo it all for fifteen years before the country said that the policies did not work or that the ideas informing such efforts were bankrupt or that black people were just "crying victim." But the black ghetto, for instance, isn't simply the result of bad black people who refuse to take on the responsibility of living full lives. Rather, the black ghetto is perhaps the best example of the value gap. White supremacy produced it.

C hanging how we see black people in this country involves changing how we see white people. If we believe that white people are valued more than others (and that belief continues to be expressed in the neighborhoods where we live, the schools we attend, and the places we work), the value gap will continue to reproduce differential outcomes in the lives of Americans. The black ghetto will become a permanent feature of American life. White Americans will continue to make excuses for why that is the case—often blaming people for their own misery—and some will continue to view racial equality as a zero-sum game.

We have to demonstrate how those habits stand in the way of democracy and distort the character of those who uncritically embrace them. James Baldwin put it plainly: "Our dehumanization of the Negro is indivisible from our dehumanization of ourselves; the loss of our own identity is the price we pay for our annulment of his."

This truth still holds today. Racial habits distort the character of those who benefit from them. Stereotypes and the stigmatization of black people fortify a particular idea of white people as somehow better than others and as representative of what is best about America. Those racial habits damage white people just as they do black people. And they don't stay in people's heads or shape only individual lives—they drive public policy. For example, the soul of America is scarred as we incarcerate a generation of black and brown people. We warehouse them in prisons, where people generate profits from them. And we have produced a culture and climate of fear—white fear of young black men and women—that justifies our indifference. A revolution of value attacks that culture at its root by changing our idea of the value of white and black people—insisting that white lives do not matter more than any other life in this country.

If we stopped seeing young black people first as criminals, we might break loose from the racial stranglehold on our national imagination. Think about the different outcomes if police changed their perception of young black people. In Philadelphia, when a group of black boys— basketball players who don't have a gym in their charter school—gets off the subway in brutally cold weather wearing hats, gloves, and scarves given to them by their teacher, the police would not see a potential crime. They would see children they should protect. We wouldn't end up with a sixteen-year-old with a ruptured testicle at the hands of a police officer. Or, beyond the police, think about a mother who might still have her daughter if Theodore Wafer had not thought Renisha McBride was trying to break into his home and shot her in the face, but instead saw someone in need of help. Sandra Bland, Eleanor Bumpers, Tanisha Anderson, and Duanna Johnson (and, tragically, so many more) might still be alive today as well.

This climate of fear forces black parents to impart particular lessons to their children. We fear for our children's lives every time they leave the relative safety of our homes, and depending upon where you live, that fear varies in intensity. I once called my son away from the comfort of his bedroom and forced him to walk outside with me. He looked stereotypically suburban: pajama bottoms, a T-shirt, and Nike running shoes. The police were at a neighbor's house. Apparently one of their boys had gotten into trouble. Instead of taking the young man to jail, they had brought him home. Even though I am a Princeton professor, I turned to *my* boy, and without blinking, I told him, "They would not have brought you home to me. They would've taken you to jail."

If we are going to change how we see black people, white people—and only white people can do this—will have to kill the idea of white people. It is the precondition of America's release into a different, democratic future. If we don't do this, we condemn ourselves to whatever tragedy awaits at the end of our current path.

I keep turning to the words of James Baldwin because, at least to me, he most vividly captures the stakes. In "Everybody's Protest Novel," he writes:

> *Now, as then, we find ourselves bound, first without, then within, by the nature of our categorization. And escape is not effected through a bitter railing against this trap; it is as though this very striving were the only motion needed to spring the trap upon us. . . .*

Society is held together by our need; we bind it together with legend, myth, coercion, fearing that without it we will be hurled into that void, within which, like the earth before the Word was spoken, the foundations of society are hidden. From this void—ourselves—it is the function of society to protect us; but it is only this void, our unknown selves, demanding, forever, a new act of creation, which can save us—"from the evil that is in the world." *(Emphasis added.)*

Baldwin understood the comfort of old ways of thinking. That our categories imposed order on an otherwise chaotic world, but that order came with a cost. We were all trapped in the very place that made us feel safe.

The belief that white people matter most is the trap. That belief, to paraphrase Susan Sontag, is the aggressive cancer of modern human history. It orders the world on the backs of black folk and fixes the place of white people in legend and myth (that for whatever reason, God or nature made white folk better than everyone else), blinding them to the humanity of others. Baldwin urges us to risk everything to escape this trap—to step outside of what is expected and see life differently. To do this, we must demand a new act of creation on the part of all of us, freed from the burdens of the idea of white people and the fears of those content with things as they are.

CHANGE WHAT MATTERS TO US AS AMERICANS

We have to tell better stories about what truly matters to us. The kinds of stories we tell reflect the kind of people—the kind of nation—we aspire to be. Bad stories, like bad habits, typically correlate with bad people. So better stories are needed to change the country. Americans have to challenge directly the idea that we are "the shining city on the hill" or "the Redeemer Nation." We have to release democracy from the burden of American exceptionalism. To do this, we have to tell stories of those who put forward a more expansive conception of American democracy. This will involve confronting the ugly side of our history, recalling the heroic and representative efforts of countless men and women who gave everything to achieve our country, and sacrificing the comfort of national innocence and the willful blindness that comes with it.

This will require a radical reordering of value. Changing our stories is a way of changing what matters. I am not suggesting that we discard the cherished notions of success and self-reliance. But a revolution of value should change what constitutes success and individual initiative. The value of human beings should never be diminished in the pursuit of profit or in the name of some ideology.

Something about the way we see the world has gone out of whack. People profit from the incarceration of millions. Corporations make money off the sick. Forty-five percent of our children live in low-income families. We have incarcerated 2.4 million Americans (the number has quadrupled since 1980). And the top 1 percent keep getting richer, while working people of all races have seen their wages stagnate; many have lost their jobs, their homes, and any hope that they might bequeath to their children a brighter future. This looks dramatically worse in black communities. And some people walk around this country as if all is well, ignorant of the moral crimes about them.

It's as if we've tossed aside any pretense to having a robust idea of the public good, because some are afraid that black people (or immigrants, or Muslims, or some other group) will threaten the advantage of white people. And that fear, along with greed and selfishness, has allowed us to let the country fall apart at the seams. One way to think about it all is that the value gap has clogged our national arteries; very little can pass through them. We're lucky that the country is still standing.

The sad thing is, we had a chance. Dr. King urged the nation to undergo a revolution of values. The United States needed to shift, he said, from "a thing-oriented society" to "a person-oriented society," to see that the gap between the rich and the poor reflected an economic order that stripped millions of people of their ability to even imagine a decent living, and to understand that war (and the monies used to execute it) put us on the road to "spiritual death." A revolution of value would demote our interests in material toys, would challenge those who believe that money rules everything, while honoring the sanctity of life and the dignity of work. As Dr. King put it, "When machines and computers, profit motives and property rights are considered more important than people, the great triplets of racism, extreme materialism, and militarism are incapable of being conquered." We have to upend our current way of valuing the world, and for me, that begins with closing the value gap.

To close that gap, black people and all of those who have turned their backs on white supremacy will have to name racism when it blocks a broader vision of the country, tell a different story when people disremember in order to justify a political agenda, and envision the beloved community in which *all* Americans do more than just go to work and tend to their individual gardens, but experience a deeply felt interdependence in a jointly shared effort to reimagine American democracy. Americans have to live together, in the deepest sense of the phrase—to make a life together that affords everyone (and I mean everyone) a real chance. This can happen only when we experience genuine connectedness, when the well-being of African Americans is bound up with any consideration of the well-being of the nation. When we are not asked to disappear, and instead have the space to reach for our best selves.

Unfortunately, the value gap and our racial habits stand in the way of any major shift in the cultural and political life of this country. Too many Americans remain committed to white privilege and are willing to defend that privilege at whatever cost. They refuse to give up the idea that white lives matter more than others. That refusal, with all its damaging effects, requires a radical response. We cannot stick our heads in the sand with the hope that *they* will finally do the right thing. We have to be boldly black, in all the complex ways our lives suggest, in the name of democracy. We have to say, without qualification, BlackLivesMatter!

Obviously, we know we matter. The phrase isn't about asserting our humanity to folks who deny it. The voices of our mighty dead shout back that the price of that ticket has been paid already. No. BlackLivesMatter reminds white people that *their* lives do not matter more than others. It is a direct challenge to white supremacy. I am reminded of the words of the African American sage W. E. B. Du Bois:

I hear his mighty cry reverberating through the world, "I am white!" Well and good, O Prometheus, divine thief! Is not the world wide enough for two colors, for many little shinings of the sun? Why, then devour your own vitals if I answer even as proudly, "I am black!"

CHAPTER NINE

RESURRECTION

had to see it for myself. Many friends and colleagues had already made their way to Ferguson before I decided to go in November of 2014. Some had participated in the #BlackLivesMatter "Freedom Ride," in which more than 500 people from cities across the country descended on Ferguson in late August and stood in solidarity with the protesters. Many would return home and organize demonstrations in their own cities. Others had gone for "Ferguson October," a call put out by clergy and activists for massive demonstrations in support of Michael Brown's family. More than a thousand protesters, some from as far away as Palestine, came "to fill Ferguson's jails as a gesture of noncompliance with a police department that they deemed morally compromised."

I thought of going, but I decided to wait until November. Reverend Osagyefo Sekou, one of the organizers of Ferguson October, gave me the names of a few key people among the protesters: folks like Tef Poe and Ashley Yates, Reverends Traci Blackmon and Renita Lamkin. He also suggested I attend a meeting of Metropolitan Congregations United (MCU) at Central Reform Congregation, a synagogue led by Rabbi Susan Talve. When I arrived, the city was standing on a knife's edge as it awaited the announcement of the grand jury.

My colleague, Joshua Guild, and I drove straight to the synagogue, where a meeting of clergy and organizers was being held. They were preparing for the grand jury decision and training people who wanted to join the protests or who volunteered their churches or synagogues to be "safe spaces" or "sanctuary churches," places where protesters could retreat and members of the community could find some comfort amid the anticipated chaos. We sat in amazement as we listened to Reverend Lamkin, a white African Methodist Episcopal minister who had been shot with rubber bullets by the Ferguson police. Her task was to rid everyone of any hint of sentimentality and to prepare them for the potential violence by the police and the intensity of the anger of the protesters.

We were given handouts. Told how to dress for the protests (layered clothing; comfortable shoes; no hoop earrings, necklaces, watches) and what to do if we got teargassed (flush our eyes with water or milk—no rubbing—and blow our noses; don't suck it back in). She urged us to protest using a buddy system. We should stay in groups of two, exchange telephone numbers, birth dates, emergency contacts, and try to have only one in the group arrested. The other would get you out of jail. She told the participants to "know their limits" and to work hard at "de-escalating" situations. There was a list of suggestions about how to interact with protesters. "Mingle, but don't ask too many personal questions; it raises suspicion." "Make eye contact with the police on the front line," but "do not talk to police!" "Avoid giving direction unless necessary for safety; never EVER tell someone 'Don't do that.' "

She was intense, and earnest. They were preparing for war.

We need a powerful expression of black politics today: everyday people engaged in concerted efforts to rebuild black communities, and movements to shake the country out of its current racial morass. We've done it before. The twentieth century is filled with examples of ordinary black folk, along with other concerned Americans, transforming our national ideas of freedom and democracy. We've paid the price too. The country's soil is soaked with the blood of black martyrs who turned their backs on the status quo and risked everything for a more expansive idea of what this country could be.

Two thousand eight was a rough and pivotal year. We have not been able to talk clearly and forcefully about the crisis in our communities without the added burden of Obama's calculated evasions of race matters and worries about giving ammunition to the right. In that sense, we haven't been able to behave like other political constituents in the democratic process, even though we voted for him at a rate of 93 percent in 2012, just four years later. At some point, we will have to ask ourselves: Was his presidency worth it all? The question is not one that awaits us in some distant future. Obama's time as president is drawing to a close, and we have to confront it now.

African Americans should not expect the next president to behave any differently than Obama has on race. If anyone cries out after 2016 about persistent racial inequality, I can imagine the response. "Where was your outrage when President Obama didn't do anything on this issue?" Accusations of a double standard will keep the black political class in check, because there will be no moral ground to stand on. Political expediency over the past eight years has eroded the soil. The political stage will have been set for a generation, unless we do something about it.

We have to turn our backs on contemporary black liberal politics. That politics gets in the way of the kind of democratic life we desperately seek. Black liberalism in its various forms today reflects the price that white supremacy demands: either we have leaders who undermine how black people participate in the democratic process, or we have to translate black experiences into more palatable, universal claims in order to maintain political consensus and continue the lie of color-blindness. Both paths support racial habits that block the way to achieving our country.

We need to do something dramatic. We must disrupt how society responds to black suffering and imagines black political participation. We also have to challenge our own sense of who and what the black community is. In other words, we need to shut down the traditional circuitry of black politics and reboot how we engage the democratic process. We need a *civic power outage,* and that will have to happen in the streets and at the ballot box. And the events in Ferguson were just the spark we needed.

FERGUSON PROTESTS

Meeting with a group of young activists showed me how the Ferguson movement was trying to change the political game. We all sat in the conference room of Teach for America in downtown St. Louis. Brittany Packnett, the executive director of TFA St. Louis, opened the space for us, and I came to learn rather quickly that she was playing a crucial role in the movement. The discussion was wide-ranging. We talked about the scale of the arbitrary violence of the police, the limits and failures of black leadership, and the organic and creative power of the protests.

Johnetta Elzie (or Netta, as she's called) caught my attention. She sat quietly at first, but then described how she was shot with rubber bullets on August 11. Two days earlier, she had gone to Canfield Drive "to pay her respects to the space, to the people, and the community." She saw Michael Brown's blood in the middle of the street, and it changed her life.

"I had on a jean jacket. I was just standing there, because we were with Wes Lowery," a reporter from the *Washington Post.* They were handing out bottled water to people when they saw three armored trucks slowly driving up the street. "They are like, 'Return to your homes.' And the people are like, 'Fuck you, you return to *your* homes. This is our home.'" Netta described how people weren't exactly in the street, just standing outside on their front lawns. They were in their neighborhood. But the police weren't having it. "So they start coming up, and the next thing you know they make an announcement: 'If you're in the streets, you're liable to get arrested.' Like it's on you." The police were about to turn it up.

"Next thing I know," Netta remembered, "I'm watching tear gas canisters get shot at people across the street, like dead at someone. It drops off the person and it explodes." Chaos ensued. "I'm watching this across the street [when] I feel like someone just punched me in the chest, and I'm like, 'What just happened to me?' Some dude, he was just checking himself, and I'm like 'What's wrong?' He says, 'We got shot.' . . . I looked down and there were rubber pellets on this man's driveway." She couldn't believe what had happened. "Oh my God, I got shot in Ferguson, for what?" she recalled thinking. "For standing on a corner trying to hand out water. And then they started teargassing us."

But Netta, the other young people, and their allies defied the police who stood in their riot gear, with long batons and M16s. "That night I wasn't concerned about the police, it became obvious to me that in order to be involved in the protests there was no place for fear," she later told a reporter from the *Huffington Post*.

The group gathered at TFA contrasted this experience with the grandstanding of the St. Louis County NAACP and other national black leaders who came to Ferguson. The NAACP had held a highly publicized mass meeting the same day Netta was shot. Local leaders and young ministers spoke passionately about the tragic death of Michael Brown and committed themselves to fight for justice on his behalf.

"It was trash," Netta murmured.

Brittany Packnett agreed. "It was just like smoke and mirrors."

The meeting wasn't organically connected to the young people in the streets. The church where the meeting was held wasn't in Ferguson, and the rhetoric, Brittany noted, was disturbing. "A lot of the rhetoric in the church was 'Well, those folks over there are the looters. We're the people who are going to find the solution over here.'"

"They were just like, 'We're the solution,'" said Netta. "I ain't seen them since."

Brittany was asked to pick up a prominent civil rights leader one day. She brought him to meet some of the key organizers on the ground and he asked, "Where are all of the people?" He wanted to be where the cameras were. "He had me take him, essentially lead a caravan, to Canfield." Some people flocked to him once they started to walk. Others, particularly those under eighteen, asked her who he was. "There was a moment where I was, like, 'This is the divide. This is it right here.'"

For the activists around the table with me, this famous civil rights leader (who I knew was the Reverend Jesse Jackson) had no real interest in the protests or the protesters or any real intention of substantively transforming the circumstances of the residents of Ferguson. He was there for himself. "I tell this story to illustrate how not to enter this place," Brittany said, "because the same person got booed when he was at a rally a couple of days later."

Larry Fellows III, another organizer, chimed in about the Reverend Sharpton and other civil rights leaders. "I know for a fact Sharpton was very critical of Ferguson October from the start. . . . He declared that he wanted to hold a march that would be more effective and much more appropriate." Sharpton approached the protests like a competition. But everyone agreed he had little, if any, influence among the people in the streets.

And the "streets" mattered. The Ferguson protesters were weary of the speeches and the grandstanding. In the name of Michael Brown, they wanted a full frontal assault on the brutality of the police and the government that supported them. None of them believed the grand jury was going to indict Darren Wilson. And they were right. But they did believe no one should be comfortable until racial justice was made real in Ferguson and in the country.

What they called "actions" made sure of that. These were often improvised acts of civil disobedience designed to disrupt business as usual. One example was called They Think It's a Game. DeRay McKesson, a Bowdoin College alum who came to Ferguson after Michael Brown's death, and Kayla Reed, an organizer for the Organization of Black Struggle, came up with the idea. One of the organizers asked what are the chances they think what the protesters are doing is a game—that it's a joke? "If they think it's a game, let's actually shut it down by playing games," Netta recalled. "Hopscotch, double Dutch, Backleg, anything you could play out in the street. . . . And shut down all of the corridors because [we're] playing games." It was brilliant.

The same group would later join up with other groups and walk toward St. Louis University, coordinating it all by word of mouth and social media. As the different groups converged on a bridge covered in fog, about 300 people confronted a line of city police officers tapping their batons against their shoes (the theater of fascist authority). Netta told the story:

> People started clapping. We can make noise too. We can sing songs. We can get on your nerves just as much as you get on ours. They don't let people pass. . . . It's like 300 people on this bridge. The people from out of town are scared. They're crying. I'm like, "What's wrong with y'all? Just be calm. We got it. . . ." We're able to go across the bridge and the crowd gets even bigger and the police still don't know what to do. And this group called Tribe X, they were the ones, us and them, we helped them with the logistics and, like, how to keep people together, but it was their idea to Occupy St. Lou. So we had Think It's a Game, Occupy St. Lou all in one night, and we just see this mass influx of people going to St. Lou, and the guard is

like, "Y'all don't have a [campus ID]." Someone in the crowd was
like, "They're actually my guests. All of them."

More than a thousand people staged an improvised sit-in on campus. This was not Sharpton's traditional march with its government permits and his $20,000 Porta-Potties. It was creative civil disobedience, which drew on the unique skill sets of this generation of activists. Leaders emerged in the moment. As Brittany put it, "Some of the most successful actions have been the ones that have been last-minute that have been planned by brilliant young people out there *in the street*, figuring out how to organize and keeping people together."

These young people engaged in acts of civil disobedience to disrupt the traditional theater of America's racial politics. No charismatic preacher stood at the front of the march. No long sermons. Just a concerted effort to force those in power to hold Darren Wilson accountable for the senseless death of Michael Brown. That specific demand came with a broader claim about how we police black communities in this country and how black people are criminalized (no matter what they are doing). In short, these young people challenged our racial habits.

The next day we met DeRay and Netta in the afternoon at Cathy's Kitchen on South Florissant. These two stood out among the protesters, because of their work with social media and the publication of the newsletter "This Is the Movement." They have chronicled the movement from the beginning, taking control of the narrative from the mainstream media. Telling their story. Tweeting anything of substance about what's happening in Ferguson. As Netta put it, "I don't need media people, because my first-day tweets to my 91-day tweets, that's what I've been doing. I was the media. So I don't need you to push me forward in front of a camera." Both were awarded the 2015 Howard

Zinn Award for their work on the newsletter and featured on the cover the *New York Times Magazine*. They are a study in contrasts. DeRay, a queer black graduate of an elite liberal arts college, is in constant motion. Sentences just flow from his mouth. Netta, a brilliant native of St. Louis, is reserved and cautious. Her brow is constantly furrowed, and she will speak her mind when necessary. Both are fearless.

DeRay described the Ferguson movement in terms of family, but it reflects a more inclusive idea of black politics. One moment in the conversation stands out. He was involved in a protest action in Shaw, a neighborhood in St. Louis. This is the place where Vonderrit Myers, an eighteen-year-old black male, was killed by an off-duty St. Louis police officer working as a security guard. The policeman maintained that Myers fired a gun at him. Witnesses say he was unarmed. DeRay described the action. "One night the police were crazy. What the police did is that they made a circle here and all the protesters got split in four directions. Two groups got trapped on the sidewalk. A group got trapped this way. . . . I got trapped on the side that was open; so we just kept moving and protesting." He then recounted this amazing moment:

> *H.J. was there and I'm like, I know him enough that we protested together. We got back to the big circle after we finished walking around and he was cursing at the police. He was like, "You fucking faggot." That's what he said to the police officer. He turns around and this other protester says, "I'm really offended by that." It happened in like twelve seconds. H.J.'s like, "I'm sorry. Everything just keeps happening. The police are macing people."*

The story revealed how complex the Ferguson movement was and is. A wide cross-section of the black community was out front in the protests. Openly queer women, for example, helped organize #BlackLivesMatter.

Alexis Templeton and Brittany Ferrell, cofounders of Millennial Activists United in Ferguson, fell in love during the protests (and later got engaged). And here in the middle of a heated action someone was willing to apologize for a hurtful homophobic remark to someone who was risking his life right beside him. As DeRay put it, "Seeing love on display in the midst of trauma is something I never would have thought I would have seen in protest."

DeRay and Netta asked Josh and me if we wanted to see the memorials for Kajieme Powell, the twenty-five-year-old man killed by St. Louis police for "lunging" at them with a knife (cell phone footage revealed that the police lied), and Vonderrit Myers. As we drove, DeRay talked about his family. His parents were drug addicts. His father had cleaned himself up, but his mother couldn't. His dad had raised him. He said it all matter-of-factly. Netta sat quietly. We arrived at the site. Without the teddy bears and stuffed animals tied to a tree, no one would have known that Powell had been killed there.

As we stood on the corner, Netta and DeRay received a tweet that an action was happening in Shaw. They looked at us and asked if we were ready. Josh and I looked intently at each other. We exchanged cell phone numbers. We wrote them down on the palms of our hands in case we lost our phones. Took off our watches and wedding rings. Agreed that only one of us would get arrested. In effect, we followed the protocols of the MCU training from a day earlier.

When we arrived in Shaw a crowd was beginning to gather near the convenience store where Myers had been killed. In one of the police accounts, the officer said Myers jumped out of the bushes and struggled with him. There were no bushes anywhere in the area. Folks mingled. Myers's father was present. DeRay and Netta immediately sprang into action. Filming and tweeting. Posting videos on Vine. Others started to come. Tef Poe of Hands Up United and the St. Louis University law professor Justin Hansford came. They, along with the parents of

Michael Brown and other activists, were preparing to leave for Geneva, Switzerland, the next morning to plead their case before the United Nations Committee against Torture. The crowd continued to grow. Close to a hundred people were now gathered on the corner.

A young man in sagging jeans and a skully began to speak with a bullhorn. He emerged as the leader of this action. "They treat us like dogs," he said. His comments ranged from criticisms of capitalism's exploitation of the ghetto to the fact that black people were once "kings and queens." It was a patchwork of analysis of the condition of the poor and most vulnerable in this society. And it didn't rely on the familiar language of nonviolence and love. He was angry. Myers's father spoke and thanked the crowd for their support. And then a cousin spoke. He stood about five feet seven with tattoos on his arms and neck. "I'm afraid to go out in these streets. Not because of some set. I can handle that. Because of the police. When I want to go to the store late at night I wake my daughter up and take her with me. Thinking maybe they won't shoot me if she's with me."

The young man grabbed the bullhorn and said, "We're not going to get arrested tonight. We're just going to let these folks know we're still here." And with that, the march began. We just followed the young folk as they marched through the neighborhood, chanting "Hands up, don't shoot" and "FTP" (fuck the police) at the top of their lungs. There were no television cameras or news reporters. No leaders at the front of the march. Just people together, walking steadily forward to keep the pressure on the powers that be. Soon the sound of helicopters above could be heard. Police cars were stationed at certain intersections. As we reached the highway, organizers told us to stay on the sidewalk. Cars followed us. They blasted rap music and young men hung out of the windows, rapping verses in honor of Vonderrit Myers. As quickly as it started, it ended. We arrived back at the corner. People hugged. They knew, for a moment, that they had disturbed the peace.

The protests in the streets of Ferguson disrupted the status quo and dramatically affected the lives of the people who live there. Some condemned the sporadic violence and challenged the effectiveness of constant demonstrations. They urged the protesters to channel their rage and turn to the ballot box. But the protests had a measurable effect. These young people exposed the predatory practices of the municipal government. The city manager and the chief of police have resigned. Police tickets have decreased. The Missouri Supreme Court called for the immediate transfer of all Ferguson municipal cases to St. Louis County. This didn't happen because of an election; it wasn't the result of aligning the demonstrations with the Democratic Party. Nor did it happen because of traditional black leadership. As one of the organizers said, "It started because regular people came outside and said enough was enough."

I don't want to romanticize it all. A lot has happened since that August. Many of the activists are now on the lecture circuit. Others have joined task forces or committees organized by government officials. Organizations have collapsed. Personal conflicts have emerged. Market forces are also doing their work. Some people have monetized their participation in the struggle. I guess it is in the nature of things. Moments of democratic awakening are fugitive. They happen in fits and starts, and rarely are sustained for extended periods of time. Democratic awakenings can, however, switch the tracks. We can find ourselves traveling down a different path because of them.

What becomes clear is that the turn to "the streets" effectively disrupted the order of things. When the protests erupted in New York after the grand jury failed to indict the cop for the death of Eric Garner—and in Chicago, Los Angeles, Oakland, Atlanta, Memphis, Miami—a shock wave was sent throughout the country. The protests put the government and traditional black leaders and organizations on notice. As Brittany Packnett put it, "We have to be serious about not allowing established people in organizations to choose comfort. We operate with authenticity to the real struggle of the people that we say we're serving." We should follow their lead. We need to stay in the streets about policing, education, and jobs with a livable wage if we are going to cut the power to the current ways of doing things and uproot the racial habits that are choking the life out of democracy.

THE BALLOT BOX

Gwen Ifill of PBS held a town hall meeting in Ferguson soon after the protests erupted. Law enforcement, government officials, thought leaders, and activists reflected on the tense days following Michael Brown's death. Tef Poe of Hands Up United expressed his loss of faith in the country. For him, and many others in the room, "the system is broken." Senator Claire McCaskill of Missouri said she understood his position, but urged him and other young black people to get involved in the political process—to run for office and, most important, to vote. Tef Poe's response was telling. "What do you say to those of us that are [politicized]? I voted for Barack Obama twice and still got teargassed." It was a stunning dismissal of the power of the ballot.

Young activists continue to face calls to translate their rage into electoral politics. To work within the system. Sharpton said as much at Michael Brown's funeral. And Ferguson protesters at the fiftieth anniversary of the Selma march were told by some older people in the crowd, "Your vote is your voice. Get registered." *New York Times* columnist Charles Blow directly challenged those who questioned the value of voting. Blow wrote, "We don't vote for people because they are the exact embodiment of our values, but because they are likely to be the most responsive to them." For him, the vote is sacred even as he recognizes how profoundly frustrating the political system is. As he put it, "We are people who must know that the voice and the vote are mutual amplifiers, not mutually exclusive."

I was talking about this question of voting with Charlene Carruthers, the national coordinator of the Black Youth Project 100, an organization that has been deeply involved in the ongoing protests around the country. She mentioned how her executive board was debating whether or not to vote at all in the next national election and what that might mean politically. She was clear about how difficult the question is: some people don't see voting as a means of change, while others "have dedicated their entire lives to expanding the franchise, of securing the franchise for black people." And the battle over the franchise for black people still rages on, 150 years after emancipation.

But if we're going to change how we participate in the democratic process in this country, we have to change how we think about "the vote." I am not suggesting that we don't vote or that we deny the value of voting. I agree with Blow. Voting and direct action are not mutually exclusive. But we need to understand voting as a tool of protest that potentially goes beyond putting people out of office.

Think about it this way: José Saramago's novel *Seeing* opens with the presiding officer of a polling station fretting over the weather. Torrential rains threaten to dampen voter turnout during a national election. No one seems to be coming to the polls. Then voters begin to show up in record numbers. But something dramatic happens. When the ballots are counted, three-quarters of them are blank. People showed up to vote, but refused to vote for any particular party. The authorities panic and call a second election. The same thing happens, except this time, 83 percent of the ballots are left unmarked. Elected officials interpret "the electoral blank-out" as a direct challenge to the democratic process.

Saramago brilliantly dramatizes a profound insight. The voters reject the choices put before them, because the entire process is bankrupt. And that refusal is a "bloodless revolutionary" act (sort of like in Melville's

Bartleby, the Scrivener: "I would prefer not to."). As "the blankers" of the capital, as they came to be called, debated the implications of their actions, one group explained succinctly what motivated them:

> [T]hey had voted the way they voted because they were disillusioned and could find no other way of making it clear just how disillusioned they were, that they could have staged a revolution, but then many people would undoubtedly have died, something they would never have wanted, that all their lives they had patiently placed their vote in the ballot box, and the results were there for all to see. This isn't democracy, sir, far from it.

Of course, this is fiction. We live in the real world. But so much of what we endure in our lives can be seen as the stuff of fiction that we may as well reach for it as a way of freeing our political imaginations.

In fact, we don't have to reach very far at all to find a blank-out campaign in our world. In 1998, Puerto Rican voters were faced with a referendum about the status of the island. They were given a choice between statehood, independence, free association, commonwealth, or none of the above. A heated debate arose over the definitions of the terms. The definition of *commonwealth*, in particular, raised some concerns. So a campaign was launched to vote "none of the above." That vote signaled a refusal to accept the given options; it was a political act to not play the game as scripted. "None of the above" won 50.2 percent of the vote.

We need to do something that bold. Something that will upset the entire game. In 2016, we should call for an "electoral blank-out." We vote in the national election for the presidency of the United States, but we leave the ballot blank or write in "none of the above." This isn't your standard call for a third-party candidate or an independent black political thrust. Nor is it a rejection of our sacred duty to vote. Exercising the franchise is sacred. Actually, I want black people to turn out for the election in record numbers *without Obama on the ticket,* but give our attention to other issues on the ballot. We should vote in congressional, state, and local elections.

Elections are important, but they are hardly the only work of democracy. For too long we've been sold a bill of goods that this person or that one will do what we need, if only we can get them elected. This promise wants us to believe that voting *is* democracy. But that's only half true. Sure, we must work overtime (sadly) to ensure that no one rolls back the gains of the Voting Rights Act and that everyone has access to the ballot. But the work of democracy does not end with elections.

We should turn our attention to efforts like the Forward Together moral movement and the Dream Defenders and #BlackLivesMatter, or to mobilizing around public school closings in our neighborhoods. Some issue, concrete and right in front of us, should be our focus. A collateral effect, although not the main objective, would be the election of men and women at the state and local levels who aren't about symbolism and celebrity, but who put forward a strategic vision for our communities. (When elections become the primary aim of grassroots mobilization, the conditions for demobilization are built into the very activity. If you succeed, you are often left twiddling your thumbs.) The hope would be that the "Blank-Out 2016" campaign could change the tone and focus of American politics, and demonstrate that black folk have finally gotten sick and tired of being sick and tired.

The core of the campaign would be a coordinated effort—*a networked coalition*—of grassroots organizations whose primary task in the run-up to the election would be to focus attention on particular issues in the black community. These organizations would urge black voters to leave the presidential ballot blank or to write "none of the above." But the trade-off would be to take up an issue (or issues) that requires our attention beyond the election cycle. The idea is to use the presidential election as a moment to disrupt the notion that democracy rests primarily with elections and to reject black liberal politics. Combined with action in the street, we could shut down the power of politics as usual in this country.

I am suggesting a seismic shift in black politics. Obviously, we can't stand idly by as Democrats take our votes for granted and cave to forces that devastate our communities. Nor can extremists on the right and those who enable them expect us to sit back as they trade in racist nonsense, continue to legislate for the 1 percent, and undo the modest gains we've made in this country. What has become crystal clear over these past few years, at least to me, is that business as usual isn't sufficient; that the typical black characters on the national scene have to be called out for what they have failed to do and say in the face of what has happened and is happening in black America.

I want to be clear. I am not suggesting that we concede the national political scene (although I am certainly suspicious of it). Instead, we have to reboot national politics—change the flow of the current. Here intensified local efforts enter into a network of other local practices across the country that, taken together, have national political implications. You can build a national politics from the ground up rather than think about it as decisions that flow from the top down. That's what the protests did. They connected what happened to Michael Brown in Missouri and Jessica Hernandez in Colorado and John Crawford III and Tanisha Anderson in Ohio with Eric Garner in New York and Trayvon Martin in Florida and Ezell Ford in California and Yvette Smith in Texas and Tony Terrell Robinson Jr. in Wisconsin. The same has happened with the reaction to the closing of schools in places like Chicago, Detroit, and Philadelphia, and with struggles for a livable wage for workers at Walmart and McDonald's all across the country.

We can do what the civil rights icon Ella Baker did, in her early days of organizing NAACP chapters. She established pathways, connections, and conduits that linked her practice across the United States. Like her, we can build a network of local efforts that can give us a more robust form of democratic politics. Collectively, such grassroots work—people doing what they do in their communities linking up with other people doing similar work in their communities—loosely constitutes a national politics.

If the nation is on fire with local movements in the streets, the Beltway has to respond. The blank-out campaign could constitute an initial dramatic act, which prefaces and follows from intensified grassroots organizing and action. If we are going to substantively address the condition of black communities and change the course of this nation, we must strategize around particular issues that cut across a number of different domains: in the courtroom (challenging voter-ID laws), at the ballot box (the blank-out campaign, running young, progressive candidates for office in local and state elections), and in the streets (constant pressure around policing, wildcat strikes about public schools, and direct action about a living wage). Imagine the combination of grassroots action, for example, about neighborhood school closings, litigation in the courts about the issue, and wildcat walkouts by students and teach-ins by teachers—all on the heels of an electoral blank-out. The traditional assumptions about black political behavior would have to be thrown out the window.

Some might say what I'm recommending amounts to electoral nihilism. We would end up giving the presidency over to Republicans and their extremist base. The Supreme Court would turn Red for the next thirty years. We would see the undoing of the health care law and the further erosion of the social safety net. And the country would be left in the hands of libertarians and corporatists, a remarkably high price to pay for *all* Americans. But these same people who shout gloom and doom fail to advocate for dramatic change to take back the country from these folks. This is the scare tactic that clouds our imaginations: that no matter the circumstances, choosing the lesser of two evils is always better. By this logic, we are imprisoned in a political cage—to accept matters as they are. I refuse to do so, because the political terrain as it is currently laid out has left black and other vulnerable communities throughout this country in shambles. I want to choose another path. I want to remake American democracy, because whatever this is, it ain't democracy.

We have to change the terms of political debate. This involves, as I have suggested, changing our view of government, our view of black and white people, and our view of what matters to us as Americans. An electoral blank-out undermines, at least for an election cycle, the assumption that black voters are captured and silent. It also disrupts the racial advocacy hustle of a black political class leveraging its ability to deliver black voters for crumbs and/or for selfish gain.

The idea of politics I'm suggesting here assumes a different kind of leadership. It insists on the capacities and responsibilities of everyday, ordinary black people and urges them to reach for a higher self even in opportunity deserts. Those deserts are fertile ground to be politically creative. They are the places in which we can think, reflect, and act anew. They provide opportunities to *expand the very idea of who matters* in the context of struggle with others and let us see ourselves as our own saviors. Ferguson showed us that. The Student Non-Violent Coordinating Committee did this in the bowels of the Deep South at the height of Jim Crow segregation. Its members dared to claim that black sharecroppers in the Mississippi Delta were not only worthy of participation in the democratic process, but they could lead themselves in doing so. We can do the same with those on the margins of our own communities—expand the *demos* to substantively include the black poor, those caught up in the criminal justice system, those who are deemed less than respectable by the folks currently in charge. Doing so, we say, loud and clear, that black lives matter and that we don't need HNICs. We simply need each other.

CONCLUSION

DEMOCRACY IN BLACK

attended the funeral of the great American poet Amiri Baraka. Controversy followed him all his life. It was part of what made him special. Haki R. Madhubuti, a renowned poet of the black arts movement
and owner of Third World Press, a black publishing company based in
Chicago, spoke at the funeral. As he delivered his heartfelt remarks, he
abruptly turned toward Baraka's coffin and said, "The Negroes are back."

It took my breath away. What could Madhubuti mean? What was it
about this moment, his memories, and their struggle together that would
lead him to say such a thing? Immediately I thought of "Uncle Toms,"
"sellouts"—those people the sociologist E. Franklin Frazier called "exaggerated Americans" who were willing to forget the wounds of the past
and conform to the demands of white people in the most minute of
details. But this was too easy. Madhubuti wasn't invoking some simple
idea of race loyalty: that somehow "Negroes" and "Uncle Toms" were
banished from power in the 1970s and have now returned triumphant.

No, Negroes referred to something more complex. I came to understand that Madhubuti was talking about the categories that set the
limits of our lives and secured the cage within which we were trapped.
Madhubuti and Baraka spent a lifetime imagining black art and culture, engaging in black politics, in ways they hoped would break the

stranglehold of that categorization. Perhaps they thought they buried "the Negro," that figment of the white imagination, for good, only to find themselves confronted in unprecedented ways by the category's overbearing presence today.

Malcolm X believed that America was in a position to have a bloodless revolution. He was not referring to a blank-out campaign. He was actually talking about the importance of the ballot: if black people "were given what the Constitution says [we were] supposed to have," we would "sweep all of the racists and the segregationists out of the country." He was wrong. Because some laws were changed, but much of our racial habits have remained. Something more basic has to happen: we have to break loose from the straitjacket of race that confines how African Americans live and how democracy is imagined in this country. That will involve turning our backs on business as usual in American politics, rejecting certain models of black leadership (a model Malcolm X often exemplifies), letting a thousand flowers of black political expression bloom (we need more than black liberals arguing among themselves), and burying, once and for all, "Negroes," "niggers," their cousins (thugs, welfare queens, absent fathers, and all the other ugly names and stereotypes), and the white people who invented them.

Calling all black people
Calling all black people, man woman child
Wherever you are, calling you, urgent, come in
Black people, come in, wherever you are, urgent calling you calling
    all black people
calling all black people, come in, black people, come on in.
—AMIRI BARAKA, "SOS"

A revolution of value could change the current course of this nation. Alongside a reimagined and reinvigorated black politics, such a plan might have a fighting chance. But we, black folk, have to change our habits too. Charlene Carruthers is the national coordinator of the Black Youth Project 100. BYP100 is composed of a hundred young black activists from across the country, who have convened to mobilize black communities beyond electoral politics. They pushed President Obama to come to Chicago to address the crisis of gun violence in the city after the death of Haidiya Pendleton, the fifteen-year-old student killed a week after performing at the president's inauguration in 2013. They were successful, but not satisfied in the least.

Carruthers has a strident criticism of the state of black politics and the habits that inform how we go about our political business. "As a young, black, queer woman, those who often are the voice and faces of what black people care about don't represent my interest." She has been an activist and an organizer for about ten years and has had an opportunity to sit at the table with traditional black organizations from the NAACP, the National Action Network, and the National Urban League. For her, "often times the most striking thing to me is what they don't do, and what they don't speak out about, because of politics in general, and more specifically because of the state of black politics—what we think is safe, what we think is feasible, and what we think is actually achievable."

If there is to be a fundamental transformation of this country and if a reimagined form of black politics is to help move us in that direction, then the narrow and limited vision of black people *among* black people has to be tossed in the garbage. When CeCe McDonald, a black trans woman, was incarcerated for defending herself during a racist, transphobic attack and revictimized by being sent to a male prison, traditional civil rights organizations were purposefully silent. It was clear, according to Carruthers, that the state had failed McDonald, but the leadership of these organizations was afraid to touch the case, because McDonald did not fit their vision of black people. "There is a fear that exists in black politics among those who are visible and those who have resources, and they are not organizing at the margins of the experiences of our people."

One of the core values of BYP100 is to be radically inclusive of all black people. The group believes that "the limited scope of who we are affects our ability and the strategies we use to actually achieve justice." Carruthers put the point powerfully:

> *Until we really, really go beyond the respectable black people or the young black man and woman who is a college graduate. . . . So we're going to lift them up because they were an A student, but also have to care about the ones who never graduated from high school or the one who was incarcerated or the one who doesn't speak well or isn't particularly eloquent or the one who doesn't follow along some gender binary. . . . Until we're able to do that, how we see justice will be limited.*

BYP100 takes a queer and feminist approach to the work of black liberation. And it does so as an "unapologetically black" organization dedicated to expanding the scope and practice of democracy. Even as it criticizes the narrow and harmful vision of black community that informs much of black political life, it does not retreat to some other category to organize and mobilize on behalf of racial justice. No translation. We don't disappear. This is an effort to reimagine black politics in light of the fullness of black humanity. Carruthers said, "I've always found myself constantly having to lift up the experiences of black people and the narratives of what needs to be challenged in this country. I've found that if I don't, there are very few people who will—or no one will at all."

BYP100 is one example, among many, of the kinds of organization and work needed to change *our* racial habits. Black people cannot be accorded special moral status because we're black. There is nothing about who we are that makes us any more capable of love and compassion, or of hatred and violence. Our stories lift up the values and virtues of "the least of these," but in our practice we often fall short. We are human beings like everyone else—just with a particular history of dealing with the deadly insecurities of white folk. The ugliness and evil that human beings are capable of can as easily be found among and between us. Insisting on the fullness of our humanity in light of all our complex differences involves, ironically enough, convincing black people of that fact too. It makes up part of the terrain of a revitalized black politics: *we* have to change our view of *ourselves*.

Young people are leading the way. Young men and women, queer and straight, are on the front lines, using Twitter, Facebook, Snapchat, and Vine, and leading this democratic awakening. They are expanding the sentiment Ella Baker voiced so powerfully in 1964: "Until the killing of black men, black mothers' sons, becomes as important to the rest of the country as the killing of a white mother's son, we who believe in freedom shall not rest." They are cutting off the power of patriarchal and homophobic understandings of black communities. All black lives matter. And until the value gap is no more, we will not rest. No one will rest.

In the end, as Amiri Baraka's poem so powerfully illustrates, the crisis engulfing our communities and the nation calls for all of us to "come out and to come on in" to work on behalf of democracy. An extraordinary challenge lies before us. Failure awaits us too. But no matter. Generations before faced their difficulties. We will face ours. With courage and the conviction that American democracy depends upon us, we will disturb the peace of the status quo and dare to imagine a new creation, a different way of being in the world. First, we must turn our backs. And we do so for a more just and democratic society.

With a revolution of value, the blank-out campaign of 2016, continued grassroots organizing, and ongoing direct action in the streets, we can set a new course for this nation. Black people have done it before. In our resistance against slavery, we offered a new path for the country. After the devastation of the Civil War, we put forward a more expansive idea of democracy as we legislated in statehouses throughout the reconstructed South. We changed the course of the nation by leaving the rural South and moving into cities in search of freedom. We connected our oppression at home with the effects of empire abroad and challenged directly U.S. foreign policy. This is the heart of democracy in black—efforts to imagine a democratic way of life without the burden of the value gap *or* the illusion that somehow this country is God's gift to the world. We have marched. We have rebelled. We have loved, and we have hated. And in each moment America has succumbed to the belief that some people are better than others because they are white.

We see this again today. There are those among us willing to turn their backs on democracy to safeguard their privilege. We won't allow it. No more sweet-talking. No more dancing. No one can be comfortable. And no individual or organization can say they alone represent black people. "We are the leaders we've been looking for." Together, we must close the value gap and uproot racial habits by doing democracy, once again, in black. If we fail this time—and if there is a God I pray that we don't—this grand experiment in democracy will be no more.

NOTES

INTRODUCTION

5 **"Negroes have proceeded from a premise"**: Martin Luther King Jr., *Where Do We Go from Here: Chaos or Community?*, p. 9.

6 **Mitt Romney declared that 47 percent**: David Korn, "Romney Tells Millionaire Donors What He Really Thinks of Obama Voters," *Mother Jones*, September 17, 2012.

7 **"a hope not hopeless but unhopeful"**: W. E. B. Du Bois, *The Souls of Black Folk*, p. 507.

9 **nearly one million black men**: See Naomi Murakawa, *The First Civil Right: How Liberals Built Prison America*, p. 1.

10 **"hope unborn had died"**: "Lift Ev'ry Voice and Sing" by James Weldon Johnson and Rosamond Johnson.

CHAPTER ONE: THE GREAT BLACK DEPRESSION

15 **According to the Federal Reserve**: Motoko Rich, "In Atlanta, Housing Woes Reflect Nation's Pain," *New York Times*, January 31, 2012.

15 **"Too many American families, too many minorities"**: "President Calls for Expanding Opportunities to Home Ownership," georgebush-whitehouse.archives.gov/news/releases/2002/06/20020617-2.html.

16 **According to the Center for Responsible Lending**: Debbie Gruenstein Bocian, Wei Li, and Keith Ernst, "Foreclosures by Race and Ethnicity: The Demographics of a Crisis," Center for Responsible Lending, June 18, 2010.

17 **"at least 10 percent of [the] 232 homes"**: Jo Becker, Sheryl Gay Stolberg, and Stephen Labaton, "Bush Drive for Home Ownership Fueled Housing Bubble," *New York Times*, December 21, 2008.

18 **lost retirement savings, which shrank by 35 percent**: Rakesh Kochar, Richard Fry, and Paul Taylor, "Wealth Gaps Rise to Record Highs

Between Whites, Blacks, Hispanics," Pew Research and Demographic Trends, July 26, 2011, http://www.pewsocialtrends.org/2011/07/26/wealth-gaps-rise-to-record-highs-between-whites-blacks-hispanics/.

19 **less than $11,746 a year:** "The State of America's Children 2014," Children's Defense Fund, http://www.childrensdefense.org/library/state-of-americas-children/2014-soac.pdf?utm_source=2014-SOAC -PDF&utm_medium=link&utm_campaign=2014-SOAC.

23 **"the oppressive lethargy of choicelessness":** Chimamanda Ngozi Adichie, *Americanah*, p. 341.

25 **nineteen of the thirty ZIP codes:** Stephanie Stamm, "Atlanta's Housing Recovery Is a Tale of Two Cities," *National Journal*, August 12, 2014.

Chapter Two: The Value Gap

32 **"politically incorrect minority":** Stan Greenberg, James Carville, and Erica Seifert, "Inside the GOP: Report on Focus Groups with Evangelical, Tea Party, and Moderate Republicans," October 7, 2013, http://www.democracycorps.com/attachments/article/954/dcor%20rpp%20 fg%20memo%20100313%20final.pdf. One summary of the focus groups: "They sense they are 'pretty white' and 'didn't go to Harvard'— we're just not [Obama]—which means they are becoming a pretty 'politically incorrect minority.' The so-called 'tolerant liberals' just aren't very tolerant when it comes to them." (13)

33 **"With the Revolution, God has shown":** Quoted in Sacvan Bercovitch, *The Rites of Assent: Transformations in the Symbolic Construction of America*, p. 39.

35 **Government keeps us safe:** Paul Ryan, *The Way Forward: Renewing the American Idea*, pp. 13, 28, 142–48.

36 **"I know a lot of people who have a lot of prejudice":** V. Dion Hayes, "Klan's Wisconsin Rally Idea Has Foes Rising to Occasion," *Chicago Tribune*, May 29, 1992.

36 **"I have now finished":** Alexis de Tocqueville, *Democracy in America*, p. 316.

39 **"The American Negro has the great advantage"**: James Baldwin, *The Fire Next Time,* p. 101.

40 **"When a man has emerged from slavery"**: Justice Bradley, Civil Rights Cases, 109 U.S. 3 (1883), https://www.law.cornell.edu/supremecourt/text/109/3.

41 **passed restrictive voter-identification laws**: Adam Liptak, "Supreme Court Invalidates Key Part of the Voting Rights Act," *New York Times,* June 25, 2013.

42 **many white Americans continue to rate**: Lawrence D. Bobo, "Somewhere Between Jim Crow & Post Racialism: Reflections on the Racial Divide in America Today," *Daedalus, The Journal of the American Academy of Arts and Sciences,* 2011, p. 28; Also see Tim Donovan, "White People Are More Racist Than They Realize," *Salon,* January 16, 2015, http://www.salon.com/2015/01/16/white_people_are _more_racist_than_they_realize_partner/.

42 **most popular answer**: Erin McClam, "Many Americans Blame 'Government Welfare' for Persistent Poverty, Poll Finds," NBC News, June 6, 2013, http://www.nbcnews.com/feature/in-plain-sight/many-americans -blame-government-welfare-persistent-poverty-poll-finds-v18802216.

43 **welfare became a problem**: Martin Gilens, *Why Americans Hate Welfare: Race, Media, and the Politics of Antipoverty Policy,* pp. 102–33.

43 **"race is the single most important predictor"**: Alberto Alesina, Edward Glaeser, and Bruce Sacerdote, "Why Doesn't the U.S. Have a European-Style Welfare State," NBER Working Paper No. 8524, October 2001, p. 4.

44 **"The idea of calling"**: Ahiza Garcia, "Ben Stein: Michael Brown Was 'Armed with His Incredibly Strong, Scary Self.'" *Talking Points Memo,* August 27, 2014, http://talkingpointsmemo.com/livewire/ben-stein-michael-brown-unarmed.

47 **she even declared**: Jillian Rayfield, "Bachmann: America Was Founded on Diversity," *Talking Points Memo,* January 24, 2011, http:// talkingpointsmemo.com/dc/bachmann-america-was-founded-on -diversity-video.

48 **between 1887 and 1906**: Stephen Tuck, *We Ain't What We Ought to Be: The Black Freedom Struggle from Emancipation to Obama,* p. 90.

49 **"People who shut"**: James Baldwin, *Notes of a Native Son,* p. 175.

Chapter Three: Racial Habits

55 **but in the choices we make and the lives we live:** Imani Perry, *More Beautiful and More Terrible: The Embrace and Transcendence of Racial Inequality,* pp. 34–41.

57 **there are places where *they* live:** Clarissa Rile Hayward, *How Americans Make Race: Stories, Institutions, Spaces,* pp. 42–80.

59 **Seventy-five percent of white Americans:** "Race and Americans' Social Networks," Public Religion Research Institute, August 28, 2014, publicreligion.org/research/2014/08/analysis-social-network/#.VcN-Y4uM9kA.

60 **This habitual way of acting:** See Nancy Ditomaso, *The American Non-Dilemma: Racial Inequality without Racism,* pp. 1–45, and Daria Roithmayr, *Reproducing Racism: How Everyday Choices Lock in White Advantage,* pp. 13–24.

60 **"Did I earn it?":** Interviews of 246 randomly selected white people from New Jersey, Ohio, and Tennessee conducted by Nancy Ditomaso, Rochelle Parks-Yancy, and Corrine Post. Quoted in their essay "White Views of Civil Rights: Color Blindness and Equal Opportunity," in *White Out: The Continuing Significance of Racism,* eds. Ashley W. Doane and Eduardo Bonilla-Silva, p. 196.

60 **"bunch of fucking lazy people":** "White Views of Civil Rights," p. 196.

61 **Americans have developed the habit of *masking*:** For a fuller discussion of masking see Kenji Yoshino, *Covering: The Hidden Assault on Our Civil Rights,* pp. 111–41.

61 **73 percent of whites:** Howard Schuman, Charlotte Steeh, Lawrence Bobo, and Maria Kryan, "Racial Attitudes in America: Trends and Interpretations," Institute of Government and Public Affairs, October 1, 2011.

61 **"You can't even talk about":** The Whiteness Project, http://www.whitenessproject.org/.

63 **So black people can endure more pain:** See Matteo Forgiarini, Marcello Galluci, and Angelo Maravita, "Racism and the Empathy for Pain on Our Skin," *Frontiers in Psychology,* vol. 2, 2011: 108.

64 **"I am trying to establish"**: Wendell Berry, *The Hidden Wound,*
p. 49.

66 **"The death of Trayvon Martin"**: Statement by the president, July 14,
2013, http://www.whitehouse.gov/the-press-office/2013/07/14/
statement-president.

67 **"You know, when"**: Remarks by the president, July 19, 2013,
http://www.whitehouse.gov/the-press-office/2013/07/19/
remarks-president-trayvon-martin.

CHAPTER FOUR: WHITE FEAR

73 **"[T]he least we can do"**: Richard Cohen, "Racism vs. Reality," *Washington Post,* July 15, 2013.

74 **"[y]ou really have"**: "Why White Fear of Murder by Blacks Is
Irrational, or Why You Shouldn't Fear the Hoody," *Daily Kos,* July 22,
2013.

75 **even if I am in no immediate danger**: See Corey Robin, *Fear: The
History of a Political Idea,* pp. 31–50; Martha C. Nussbaum, *Political
Emotions: Why Love Matters for Justice,* pp. 314–77; Zygmunt Bauman, *Liquid Fear,* pp. 1–21.

76 **"[T]he world has accepted the story"**: Ida B. Wells-Barnett, *The Red
Record: Tabulated Statistics and Alleged Causes of Lynching in the
United States.*

76 **a fear just waiting to be expressed**: Robert Nozick, "Prohibition, Compensation, and Risk," in *Anarchy, State, and Utopia,* pp. 54–87.

76 *racial moral panics*: Cathy Cohen, *Democracy Remixed: Black Youth
and the Future of American Politics,* pp. 18–49.

77 **"going to see a white lady"**: Martha Hodes, "The Sexualization of
Reconstruction Politics: White Women and Black Men in the South
after the Civil War," *Journal of the History of Sexuality,* vol. 3, no. 3:
407–8. Also see *Report of the Joint Select Committee to Inquire into
the Condition of Affairs in the Late Insurrectionary States* (42nd
Congress, 1872), vol. 6: 356–63; see also pp. 430–31.

77 **"a wave of terror"**: Strom Thurmond, *Congressional Record,* 1959: 18382.

77 **"The growing menace"**: Barry Goldwater, "Acceptance Speech of the Republican Presidential Nomination," July 16, 1964, http://www .americanrhetoric.com/speeches/barrygoldwater1964rnc.htm.

78 **"thirty thousand more young muggers"**: James C. Howell, "Super-predators and Other Myths about Juvenile Delinquency," in *Preventing and Reducing Juvenile Deliquency,* p. 4.

79 **"If I knew then what I know now"**: Elizabeth Becker, "As Ex-Theorist on Young 'Superpredators,' Bush Aide Regrets," *New York Times,* February 9, 2001.

79 **"This fear is general"**: Philip Fisher, *The Vehement Passions,* p. 110.

81 ***"Well, people are gonna perceive you as a menace"***: "Fox's Geraldo Rivera: 'I Think the Hoodie Is as Much Responsible for Trayvon Martin's Death as George Zimmerman,'" *Media Matters,* March 23, 2012.

81 **black participants were more inclined:** Joshua Correll, Bernadette Park, Charles Judd, and Berd Wittenbrink, "The Police Officer's Dilemma: Using Ethnicity to Disambiguate Potentially Threatening Individuals," *Journal of Personality and Social Psychology,* vol. 83, no. 6 (2002): pp. 1,314–29.

84 **"Indeed I tremble for my country"**: Thomas Jefferson, *Notes on the State of Virginia,* p. 174.

84 **"The whole commerce"**: Ibid.

85 **"The parent storms"**: Ibid.

85 **"Fondly do we hope"**: Abraham Lincoln, Second Inaugural Address, http://www.bartleby.com/124/pres32.html.

87 **"This breeds paranoia"**: Ross Douthat, "The Roots of White Anxiety," *New York Times,* July 18, 2010.

87 **"It's my honest opinion"**: The Whiteness Project, "Harold," http:// www.whitenessproject.org/checkbox/harold.

88 **ANTI-RACISM IS A CODE WORD FOR ANTI-WHITE:** Travis Gettys, "Knoxville Drivers Greeted by Banners Warning That Diversity Is Anti-White Genocide," *RawStory,* December 31, 2013, http://www

.rawstory.com/rs/2013/12/knoxville-drivers-greeted-by-banners
-warning-that-diversity-is-anti-white-genocide/.

89 **"[A] similar anger exists":** Barack Obama, "A More Perfect Union,"
Speech on Race at the National Constitution Center, March 18, 2008,
http://constitutioncenter.org/amoreperfectunion/.

90 **"If we're honest with ourselves":** President Obama Marks the 50th Anniversary of the March on Washington, August 28, 2013, https://www
.whitehouse.gov/photos-and-video/video/2013/08/28/president-obama
-marks-50th-anniversary-march-washington.

CHAPTER FIVE: RESTLESS SLEEP AFTER KING'S DREAM

98 **Grown men descended upon:** Taylor Branch, *At Canaan's Edge:
America in the King Years 1965–68*, pp. 526–29.

101 **the fragment of his body of work:** See Michael Eric Dyson, *I May
Not Get There with You: The True Martin Luther King, Jr.*,
pp. 1–10.

102 **"We have found one another again":** Quoted in David Blight, *Race
and Reunion: The Civil War in American Memory,* p. 11; "Address at
the Gettysburg Battlefield," July 4, 1913, in Arthur S. Link, ed., *Papers
of Woodrow Wilson* (Princeton: Princeton University Press), vol. 28:
23–25.

103 **"The 1913 'Peace Jubilee'":** *Race and Reunion,* p. 9.

104 **"I believe in people":** Ronald Reagan's Neshoba County Fair Speech,
August 3, 1980, http://neshobademocrat.com/main.asp?SectionID
=2&SubSectionID=297&ArticleID=15599.

105 **"We have frequently printed the word Democracy":** "Democratic
Vistas," in *The Portable Walt Whitman,* p. 348.

105 **"Now our nation":** Ronald Reagan, "Remarks on Signing the Bill
Making the Birthday of Martin Luther King, Jr. a National Holiday,"
November 2, 1983, http://www.presidency.ucsb.edu/ws/?pid=40708.

107 **"If the law can be disregarded":** Young Americans for Freedom,
"King Was a Collectivist" (1968), in Donald T. Critchlow and Nancy

MacLean, *Debating the American Conservative Movement, 1945 to the Present,* p. 191.

107 **"What conservatives wanted now"**: Daniel T. Rodgers, *The Age of Fracture,* p. 128.

108 **"The new racism"**: Quoted in *The Age of Fracture,* p. 133.

110 **"If [Martin Luther King]"**: Bill Clinton's speech in Memphis, November 13, 1993, http://www.presidentialrhetoric.com/historicspeeches/clinton/memphis.html.

112 **"Power cannot compel it"**: Bill Clinton's Commencement Address at the University of California San Diego, in *One America in the 21st Century: Forging a New Future,* p. 133.

113 **"We see a disturbing tendency"**: *One America in the 21st Century,* p. 134.

114 **"What do I really hope"**: *One America in the 21st Century,* p. 139.

115 **"That is the unfinished work of our time"**: Ibid.

CHAPTER SIX: BETWEEN TWO WORLDS

122 **"the specific conflict"**: Charles Johnson, "The End of the Black American Narrative," *The American Scholar,* Summer 2008.

123 **"blacks can still be thought of as a single race"**: "Optimism About Black Progress Declines: Blacks See Growing Values Gap Between Poor and Middle Class," Pew Research Center, November 13, 2007; Eugene Robinson, *Disintegration: The Splintering of Black America,* pp. 1–24.

127 **We're now full-fledged Americans**: Robert Putnam, *Bowling Alone: The Collapse and Revival of American Community.*

127 **what social scientists call "free spaces"**: Sara Evans and Harry C. Boyte, *Free Spaces: The Sources of Democratic Change in America*; Cathy Cohen and Michael Dawson, "Neighborhood Poverty and African American Politics," *American Political Science Review,* vol. 87, no. 2 (June 1993), pp. 286–302.

129 **institutionally rudderless**: Fredrick Harris, "Will the Circle Be Unbroken? The Erosion and Transformation of African American

Civic Life," *Philosophy and Public Policy Quarterly* 18, no. 3 (1998).

132 **"Parent PLUS loans dropped by 45 percent"**: "The Parent PLUS Loan Crisis: An Urgent Crisis Facing Students at the Nation's HBCUs," UNCF, http://www.uncf.org/sites/advocacy/SpecialInitiatives/Parents Plus/MediaDocuments/UNCF-Report-THE-PARENT-PLUS-LOAN -CRISIS-3.25.14.pdf.

133 **"In other words"**: Jarrett Carter, "Report: President Obama Criticizes HBCUs in Meeting with CBC," *HBCU Digest,* February 13, 2015.

137 **"You are not sitting in this church"**: Bernice King's Eulogy of Coretta Scott King, February 7, 2006.

137 **Bernice King lit a torch**: Jonathan Walton, *Watch This! The Ethics and Aesthetics of Black Televangelism,* pp. 125–26.

138 **"Many people think"**: Creflo Dollar, "The Gospel to the Poor," https:// creflodollarministries.org/BibleStudy/StudyNotes.aspx?id=997.

140 **"is not a human or a personal reality"**: James Baldwin, *The Fire Next Time,* p. 104.

CHAPTER SEVEN: PRESIDENT OBAMA AND BLACK LIBERALS

146 **"This was maybe America's last chance"**: Chris Hedges, "The Obama Deception: Why Cornel West Went Ballistic," *Truthdig,* May 16, 2011, http://www.truthdig.com/report/page2/the_obama_deception_why _cornel_west_went_ballistic_20110516.

147 **"I am new enough"**: Barack Obama, *The Audacity of Hope: Thoughts on Reclaiming the American Dream,* p. 12.

149 **"Those who do not believe"**: Quoted in David Caute, *The Great Fear: The Anti-Communist Purge Under Truman and Eisenhower,* p. 15.

151 **"The values of self-reliance"**: *The Audacity of Hope,* p. 54.

154 **"My own feeling"**: Rebecca Shad, "Rep. Lewis to Obama: Declare Martial Law," *The Hill,* August 14, 2014, http://thehill.com/blogs/ blog-briefing-room/215151-rep-lewis-obama-should-declare-martial -law-in-ferguson.

155 **"The Americans who crossed this bridge"**: President Obama's Speech

Celebrating the 50th Anniversary of the March on Selma, March 7, 2015, http://time.com/3736357/barack-obama-selma-speech-transcript/.

156 **"An emphasis":** *The Audacity of Hope*, p. 247.

157 **"The Negro graduates of Fisk University":** Ralph J. Bunche, "The Barriers of Race Can Be Surmounted," Commencement Address at Fisk University, Nashville, Tennessee, May 30, 1949, http://www.blackpast .org/1949-ralph-j-bunche-barriers-race-can-be-surmounted.

158 **"[I]t has a certain truth":** W. E. B. Du Bois, "The Criteria of Negro Art," *The Crisis*, vol. 32 (October 1926): 290–97.

159 **"Your country?":** *The Souls of Black Folk*, p. 549.

161 **"A reign of terror":** See Walter White, *A Man Called White: The Autobiography of Walter White*, pp. 322–23; Carol Anderson, *Eyes off the Prize: The United Nations and the African American Struggle for Human Rights, 1944–1955*, pp. 58–60; Mary Dudziak, *Cold War Civil Rights: Race and the Image of Democracy*, pp. 18–26; Donald R. McCoy and Richard T. Ruetten, *Quest and Response: Minority Rights and the Truman Administration*, pp. 45–48.

161 **They wanted to see their senators:** "Aroused by Lynchings, Women's Group Pickets," *The Afro American*, August 16, 1946.

161 **"to throw the full force of the federal government":** *Quest and Response: Minority Rights and the Truman Administration*, p. 46.

162 **"This swelling wave":** Martin Duberman, *Paul Robeson: A Biography*, pp. 305–6.

163 **"foreign intervention":** *Quest and Response*, pp. 48–49.

163 **racial justice:** Penny Von Eschen, *Race Against Empire: Black Americans and Anti-Colonialism, 1937–1957*, pp. 110–14.

164 **"Are we to be one people":** Barbara Jordan's Keynote Address at the 1976 Democratic National Convention, http://www.americanrhetoric .com/speeches/barbarajordan1976dnc.html.

165 **"to the total society":** Charles V. Hamilton, "Full Employment as a Viable Issue," in Andrew F. Brimmer, *When the Marching Stopped: An Analysis of Black Issues in the '70s*, pp. 87–91; Charles V. Hamilton, "De-racialization: Examination of a Political Strategy," in *First World: International Journal of Black Political Thought* (March–April 1977), pp. 3–5.

166 **deracialization had become a strategy:** Fredrick C. Harris, *The Price of the Ticket: Barack Obama and the Rise and Decline of Black Politics*, pp. 170–92.

168 **"We do not have a single leader":** Sheila Rule, "Black Caucus in Capital Works to Develop Communal Leadership," *New York Times*, September 30, 1981.

169 **"the embodiment of collective black aspirations!":** Adolph Reed Jr., *The Jesse Jackson Phenomenon: The Crisis of Purpose in Afro-American Politics*, p. 5.

172 **"tired rant":** Juan Williams, *Enough: The Phony Leaders, Dead-End Movements, and the Culture of Failure That Are Undermining Black America—And What We Can Do About It*, p. 32.

172 **"a moral manipulation":** Shelby Steele, *Shame: How America's Past Sins Have Polarized Our Country*, p. 37.

174 **Troubled Asset Relief Program (TARP) funds:** "Economy Tops Agenda as Obama Meets with African-American Leaders," CNN.com, February 10, 2010, http://www.cnn.com/2010/POLITICS/02/10/obama.african.americans/.

Chapter Eight: A Revolution of Value

181 **"If I didn't exist, they'd have to invent me":** Eli Saslow, "The Public and Private Doubts of Al Sharpton," *Washington Post*, February 7, 2015.

183 **"to widen the circle":** Statement by President Obama, July 14, 2013, https://www.whitehouse.gov/the-press-office/2013/07/14/statement-president.

188 **ignore how we exported our racism:** C. Vann Woodward makes this point in his classic book *The Strange Career of Jim Crow*. "Then, in the year 1898, the United States plunged into imperialistic adventures overseas under the leadership of the Republican Party. These adventures in the Pacific and Caribbean suddenly brought under the jurisdiction of the United States some eight million people of the colored races, 'a varied assortment of inferior races, as the Nation described them, which, of course, could not be allowed to vote.'" (p. 72)

190 **"The very idea of democracy"**: John Dewey, "The Challenge of Democracy to Education," in *John Dewey: The Later Works, 1925– 1953*, vol. 11: p. 182.

191 **"We started this"**: Lou DuBose, "The Politics of Faith and Fusion: Moral Monday in North Carolina," *Washington Spectator*, January 6, 2014.

194 **Five demands:** For a fuller account of the five demands, see William J. Barber II (with Barbara Zelter), *Forward Together: A Moral Message for the Nation.*

200 **"Our dehumanization of the Negro"**: James Baldwin, "Many Thousands Gone," in *Notes of a Native Son*, p. 25.

201 **"Now, as then"**: James Baldwin, "Everybody's Protest Novel," in *Notes of a Native Son*, p. 20.

204 **"When machines and computers"**: Martin Luther King Jr., "Beyond Vietnam," April 4, 1967, http://mlk-kpp01.stanford.edu/index.php/encyclopedia/documentsentry/doc_beyond_vietnam/.

205 **"I hear his mighty cry"**: W. E. B. Du Bois, "The Souls of White Folk," in *Darkwater: The Twentieth Century Completion of Uncle Tom's Cabin*, p. 52.

CHAPTER NINE: RESURRECTION

209 **"to fill Ferguson's jails"**: Jelani Cobb, "Ferguson October: A Movement Goes on Offense," *The New Yorker*, October 15, 2014, http://www.newyorker.com/news/news-desk/ferguson-october.

221 **"We are people"**: Charles Blow, "America, Who Are We?," *New York Times*, December 14, 2014.

223 **"[T]hey had voted the way they voted"**: José Saramago, *Seeing*, p. 90.

223 **"None of the above"**: Mireya Navarro, "Looking Beyond Vote in Puerto Rico After 'None of the Above' is Top Choice," *New York Times*, December 15, 1998.

226 **what I'm recommending:** Michele Goldberg, "Adolph Reed and Electoral Nihilism," *The Nation*, March 3, 2014.

Notes

Conclusion

231 **"exaggerated Americans"**: E. Franklin Frazier, *Black Bourgeoisie,*
p. 193.

232 **if black people:** Malcolm X, "The Black Revolution," in *Malcolm X
Speaks,* p. 57.

232 **"Calling all black people"**: Amiri Baraka, "SOS," in Amiri Baraka and
William J. Harris, *The Leroi Jones/Amiri Baraka Reader,* p. 218.

SUGGESTED READING

These are the books that informed my writing of *Democracy in Black*. They offer a more in-depth treatment of the topic of racial inequality and American politics today. Most are academic books. But any interested reader, with discipline and grit, can tackle this topic. Think of it as a preliminary reading list on the subject.

Abrajano, Maris, and Zoltan L. Hajnal. *White Backlash: Immigration, Race, and American Politics*. Princeton: Princeton University Press, 2015.

Adichie, Chimamanda Ngozi. *Americanah*. New York: Anchor, 2014.

Alexander, Michelle. *The New Jim Crow: Mass Incarceration in the Age of Color Blindness*. New York: The New Press, 2012.

Allen, Danielle S. *Talking to Strangers: Anxieties of Citizenship since Brown v. Board of Education*. Chicago: University of Chicago Press, 2004.

Alterman, Eric, and Kevin Mattson. *The Cause: The Fight for American Liberalism from Franklin Roosevelt to Barack Obama*. New York: Viking, 2012.

Anderson, Carol. *Bourgeois Radicals: The NAACP and the Struggle for Colonial Liberation, 1941–1960*. Cambridge: Cambridge University Press, 2015.

———. *Eyes off the Prize: The United Nations and the African American Struggle for Human Rights, 1944–1955*. Cambridge: Cambridge University Press, 2003.

Anderson, Elizabeth. *The Imperative of Integration*. Princeton: Princeton University Press, 2010.

Armour, Jody David. *Negrophobia and Reasonable Racism: The Hidden Costs of Being Black in America*. New York: New York University Press, 1997.

Baldwin, James. *The Fire Next Time*. New York: Vintage, 1963.

———. *Notes of a Native Son*. Boston: Beacon Press, 1955.

Banaji, Mahzarin R., and Anthony G. Greenwald. *Blind Spot: Hidden Biases of Good People*. New York: Delacorte Press, 2013.

Suggested Reading

Baraka, Amiri, and William J. Harris. *The Leroi Jones/Amiri Baraka Reader.* New York: Basic Books, 1999.

Barber II, William J., with Barbara Zelter. *Forward Together: A Moral Message for the Nation.* St. Louis: Chalice Press, 2014.

Bartels, Larry M. *Unequal Democracy: The Political Economy of the New Gilded Age.* New York: Russell Sage Foundation, 2008.

Bauman, Zygmunt. *Liquid Fear.* Malden, Mass.: Polity Press, 2006.

Bercovitch, Sacvan. *The Rites of Assent: Transformations in the Symbolic Construction of America.* New York: Routledge, 1993.

Berry, Wendell. *The Hidden Wound.* Berkeley: Counterpoint, 2010.

Blight, David. *Race and Reunion: The Civil War in American Memory.* Cambridge: Harvard Belknap, 2001.

Branch, Taylor. *At Canaan's Edge: America in the King Years 1965–68.* New York: Simon & Schuster, 2006.

Brimmer, Andrew F. *When the Marching Stopped: An Analysis of Black Issues in the '70s.* National Urban League, 1973.

Brown, Michael K., Martin Carnoy, Elliott Currie, Troy Duster, David B. Oppenheimer, Marjorie M. Shultz, and David Welman, eds. *White-Washing Race: The Myth of a Color-Blind Society.* Berkeley: University of California Press, 2003.

Brown, Wendy. *Undoing the Demos: Neoliberalism's Stealth Revolution.* New York: Zone Books, 2015.

Caute, David. *The Great Fear: The Anti-Communist Purge Under Truman and Eisenhower.* New York: Simon & Schuster, 1978.

Cavarero, Adriana. *Relating Narratives: Storytelling and Selfhood.* Translated by Paul Kottman. London: Routledge, 2000.

Cohen, Cathy. *Democracy Remixed: Black Youth and the Future of American Politics.* New York: Oxford University Press, 2012.

Collins, Patricia Hill. *Black Feminist Thought: Knowledge, Consciousness, and Empowerment.* New York: Routledge, 2008.

———. *Fighting Words: Black Women and the Search for Justice.* Minneapolis: University of Minnesota Press, 1998.

Crespino, Joseph. *In Search of Another Country: Mississippi and the Conservative Counterrevolution.* Princeton: Princeton University Press, 2007.

Critchlow, David, and Nancy MacLean. *Debating the American Conservative*

Movement, 1945 to the Present. Lanham, Md.: Rowman & Littlefield, 2009.

Dardot, Pierre, and Christian Laval. *The New Way of the World: On Neo-Liberal Society.* Translated by Gregory Elliot. London: Verso, 2013.

Davidson, Cathy N. *Now You See It: How Technology and Brain Science Will Transform Schools and Business for the 21st Century.* New York: Penguin, 2011.

Dawson, Michael C. *Blacks in and out of the Left.* Cambridge: Harvard University Press, 2013.

———. *Black Visions: The Roots of Contemporary African American Political Ideologies.* Chicago: University of Chicago Press, 2001.

———. *Not in Our Lifetimes: The Future of Black Politics.* Chicago: University of Chicago Press, 2011.

Dewey, John. *Human Nature and Conduct.* New York: Henry Holt and Company, 1922.

———. *The Public and Its Problems.* New York: Henry Holt and Company, 1927.

Ditomaso, Nancy. *The American Non-Dilemma: Racial Inequality without Racism.* New York: Russell Sage, 2012.

Doane, Ashley W., and Eduardo Bonilla-Silva, eds. *White Out: The Continuing Significance of Racism.* New York: Routledge, 2003.

Duberman, Martin. *Paul Robeson: A Biography.* New York: Alfred Knopf, 1989.

Du Bois, W. E. B. *The Souls of Black Folk.* Chicago: A. C. McClurg & Co., 1903.

———. *Darkwater: The Twentieth Century Completion of "Uncle Tom's Cabin."* Washington, D.C.: Austin Jenkins Co., 1920.

Duhigg, Charles. *The Power of Habit: Why We Do What We Do in Life and Business.* New York: Random House, 2012.

Dyson, Michael Eric. *I May Not Get There with You: The True Martin Luther King, Jr.* New York: Free Press, 2001.

Evans, Sara, and Harry C. Boyte. *Free Spaces: The Sources of Democratic Change in America.* Chicago: University of Chicago Press, 1992.

Feagin, Joe R. *The White Racial Frame: Centuries of Racial Framing and Counter-Framing.* New York: Routledge, 2010.

Fenno, Richard. *Going Home: Black Representatives and Their Constituents.* Chicago: University of Chicago Press, 2003.

Fisher, Philip. *The Vehement Passions.* Princeton: Princeton University Press, 2003.

Frank, Thomas. *What's the Matter with Kansas? How Conservatives Won the Heart of America.* New York: Henry Holt, 2004.

Frankenberg, Ruth. *White Women, Race Matters: The Social Construction of Whiteness.* Minneapolis: University of Minnesota, 1993.

Frazier, E. Franklin. *Black Bourgeoisie.* New York: Collier Books, 1962.

Frymer, Paul. *Uneasy Alliances: Race and Party Competition in America.* Princeton: Princeton University Press, 1999.

Garrow, David. *The FBI and Martin Luther King, Jr.* New Haven, Conn.: Yale University Press, 2006.

Gilens, Martin. *Why Americans Hate Welfare: Race, Media, and the Politics of Antipoverty Policy.* Chicago: University of Chicago Press, 2000.

Gillespie, Andra, ed. *Whose Black Politics? Cases in Post-Racial Black Leadership.* New York: Routledge, 2010.

Gilliom, John. *Overseers of the Poor: Surveillance, Resistance and the Limits of Privacy.* Chicago: University of Chicago Press, 2001.

Glaude Jr., Eddie S. *In a Shade of Blue: Pragmatism and the Politics of Black America.* Chicago: University of Chicago Press, 2007.

Goodwin, Joanne L. *Gender and the Politics of Welfare Reform: Mother's Pensions in Chicago 1911–1929.* Chicago: University of Chicago Press, 1996.

Gottesdiener, Laura. *A Dream Foreclosed: Black America and the Fight for a Place to Call Home.* Westfield, N.J.: Zuccotti Park Press, 2013.

Guinier, Lani, and Gerald Torres. *The Miner's Canary: Enlisting Race, Resisting Power, Transforming Democracy.* Cambridge: Harvard University Press, 2002.

Hanchard, Michael. *Party/Politics: Horizons in Black Political Thought.* New York: Oxford University Press, 2006.

Harcourt, Bernard E. *Illusion of Order: The False Promise of Broken Windows Policing.* Cambridge: Harvard University Press, 2001.

Harris, Fredrick C. *The Price of the Ticket: Barack Obama and the Rise and Decline of Black Politics.* New York: Oxford University Press, 2012.

Suggested Reading

Harris, Fredrick C., and Robert C. Lieberman, eds. *Beyond Discrimination: Racial Inequality in a Postracist Era.* New York: Russell Sage Foundation, 2013.

Hayward, Clarissa Rile. *How Americans Make Race: Stories, Institutions, Spaces.* Cambridge: Cambridge University Press, 2013.

Henry, C. Michael, ed. *Race, Poverty, and Domestic Policy.* New Haven, Conn.: Yale University Press, 2004.

Higginbotham, F. Michael. *Ghosts of Jim Crow: Ending Racism in Post-Racial America.* New York: New York University Press, 2013.

Hollinger, David. *Postethnic America: Beyond Multiculturalism.* New York: Basic Books, 1997.

Holloway, Jonathan Scott. *Jim Crow Wisdom: Memory & Identity in Black America since 1940.* Chapel Hill: University of North Carolina Press, 2013.

Howell, James C. *Preventing and Reducing Juvenile Delinquency.* New York: Sage Publications, 2008.

Huggins, Nathan, ed. *W. E. B. Du Bois: Writings.* New York: The Library of America, 1986.

Iacoboni, Marco. *Mirroring People: The New Science of How We Connect with Others.* New York: Farrar, Straus and Giroux, 2008.

Ifill, Gwen. *The Breakthrough: Politics and Race in the Age of Obama.* New York: Anchor, 2009.

Jackson, John L. *Real Black: Adventures in Racial Sincerity.* Chicago: University of Chicago Press, 2005.

Jacobson, Matthew Frye. *Whiteness of a Different Color: European Immigrants and the Alchemy of Race.* Cambridge: Harvard University Press, 1998.

Johnson, Cedric. *Revolutionaries to Race Leaders: Black Power and the Making of African American Politics.* Minneapolis: University of Minnesota Press, 2007.

Johnson, Cedric, ed. *The Neoliberal Deluge: Hurricane Katrina, Late Capitalism, and the Remaking of New Orleans.* Minneapolis: University of Minnesota Press, 2011.

Kelley, Robin D. G. *Freedom Dreams: The Black Radical Imagination.* Boston: Beacon Press, 2003.

Suggested Reading

Kennedy, Randall. *The Persistence of the Color Line: Racial Politics and the Obama Presidency.* New York: Pantheon, 2011.

———. *Sellout: The Politics of Racial Betrayal.* New York: Vintage, 2008.

Kinder, Donald R., and Lynn Sanders. *Divided by Color: Racial Politics and Democratic Ideals.* Chicago: University of Chicago Press, 1997.

King Jr., Martin Luther. *Where Do We Go from Here: Chaos or Community?* New York: Harper & Row, 1967.

Kruse, Kevin. *White Flight: Atlanta and the Making of Modern Conservatism.* Princeton: Princeton University Press, 2005.

Lamont, Michele, and Marcel Fournier, eds. *Cultivating Differences: Symbolic Boundaries and the Making of Inequality.* Chicago: University of Chicago Press, 1992.

Lang, Charles. *Black America in the Shadow of the Sixties: Notes on the Civil Rights Movement, Neoliberalism, and Politics.* Ann Arbor: University of Michigan Press, 2015.

Lassiter, Matthew D. *The Silent Majority: Suburban Politics in the Sunbelt South.* Princeton: Princeton University Press, 2006.

Lassiter, Matthew D., and Joseph Crespino. *The Myth of Southern Exceptionalism.* New York: Oxford University Press, 2010.

Lebron, Christopher J. *The Color of Our Shame: Race and Justice in Our Time.* New York: Oxford University Press, 2013.

Lipset, Seymour Martin. *American Exceptionalism: A Double-Edged Sword.* New York: W. W. Norton & Company, 1996.

Lipsitz, George. *The Possessive Investment in Whiteness: How White People Profit from Identity Politics.* Philadelphia: Temple University Press, 2006.

Lopez, Ian. *Dog Whistle Politics: How Coded Racial Appeals Have Reinvented Racism and Wrecked the Middle Class.* New York: Oxford University Press, 2015.

Lowenthal, David. *The Past Is a Foreign Country.* Cambridge: Cambridge University Press, 1985.

Lowndes, Joseph. *From the New Deal to the New Right: Race and the Southern Origins of Modern Conservatism.* New Haven, Conn.: Yale University Press, 2008.

Lowndes, Joseph, Julie Novkov, and Dorian T. Warren, eds. *Race and American Political Development*. New York: Routledge, 2008.

Lowry, Glenn. *The Anatomy of Racial Inequality*. Cambridge: Harvard University Press, 2002.

Malcolm X. *Malcolm X Speaks*. Edited by George Breitman. New York: Grove Press, 1965.

Manza, Jeff, and Christopher Uggen. *Locked Out: Felon Disenfranchisement and American Democracy*. New York: Oxford University Press, 2006.

Marable, Manning. *Living Black History: How Reimagining the African American Past Can Remake America's Racial Future*. New York: Basic Books, 2006.

———. *Race, Reform, and Rebellion: The Second Reconstruction in Black America, 1945–1990*. Jackson: University Press of Mississippi, 1991.

Massey, Douglass. *Categorically Unequal: The American Stratification System*. New York: Russell Sage Foundation, 2008.

Massey, Douglass, and Nancy Denton. *American Apartheid: Segregation and the Making of the Underclass*. Cambridge: Harvard University Press, 1998.

McCoy, Donald R., and Richard T. Ruetten. *Quest and Response: Minority Rights and the Truman Administration*. Lawrence: University Press of Kansas, 1973.

McWhorter John. *Losing the Race: Self-Sabotage in Black America*. New York: Harper Perennial, 2001.

Morris, Aldon D. *The Origins of the Civil Rights Movement: Black Communities Organizing for Change*. New York: Free Press, 1984.

Murakawa, Naomi. *The First Civil Right: How Liberals Built Prison America*. New York: Oxford University Press, 2014.

Myers, Kristen. *Racetalk: Racism Hiding in Plain Sight*. New York: Rowman and Littlefield, 2005.

Nozick, Robert. *Anarchy, State and Utopia*. New York: Basic Books, 2013.

Nussbaum, Martha C. *Political Emotions: Why Love Matters for Justice*. Cambridge: Belknap Press, 2013.

Obama, Barack. *The Audacity of Hope: Thoughts on Reclaiming the American Dream*. New York: Crown Publishers, 2006.

Suggested Reading

O'Connell, Brian. *Civil Society: The Underpinnings of American Democracy.* Hanover, N.H.: University Press of New England, 1999.

Olson, Joel. *The Abolition of White Democracy.* Minneapolis: University of Minneapolis Press, 2004.

Omi, Michael, and Howard Winant. *Racial Formation in the United States.* New York: Routledge, 2015.

Packer, George. *The Unwinding: An Inner History of the New America.* New York: Farrar, Straus and Giroux, 2013.

Pager, Devah. *Marked: Race, Crime, and Finding Work in an Era of Mass Incarceration.* Chicago: University of Chicago Press, 2007.

Painter, Nell. *The History of White People.* New York: W. W. Norton & Company, 2011.

Payne, Charles. *I've Got the Light of Freedom: The Organizing Tradition and the Mississippi Freedom Struggle.* Berkeley: University of California Press, 1995.

Perry, Imani. *More Beautiful and More Terrible: The Embrace and Transcendence of Racial Inequality.* New York: New York University Press, 2011.

Pettit, Philip. *Republicanism: A Theory of Freedom and Government.* Oxford: Oxford University Press, 1997.

Putnam, Robert. *Bowling Alone: The Collapse and Revival of American Community.* New York: Touchstone, 2001.

———. *Making Democracy Work.* Princeton: Princeton University Press, 1993.

Rankine, Claudine. *Citizen: An American Lyric.* Minneapolis: Graywolf Press, 2014.

Ransby, Barbara. *Ella Baker and the Black Freedom Movement.* Chapel Hill: University of North Carolina Press, 2003.

Reed Jr., Adolph. *The Jesse Jackson Phenomenon: The Crisis of Purpose in Afro-American Politics.* New Haven, Conn.: Yale University Press, 1986.

———. *Stirrings in the Jug: Black Politics in the Post-Segregation Era.* Minneapolis: University of Minnesota Press, 1999.

———. *Without Justice for All: The New Liberalism and Our Retreat from Racial Equality.* Boulder, Colo.: Westview Press, 1999.

Rigueur, Leah Wright. *The Loneliness of the Black Republican*. Princeton: Princeton University Press, 2015.

Riley, Jason. *Please Stop Helping Us: How Liberals Make It Harder for Blacks to Succeed*. New York: Encounter Books, 2014.

Roberts, Dorothy. *Shattered Bonds: The Color of Child Welfare*. New York: Basic Books, 2002.

Robin, Corey. *Fear: The History of a Political Idea*. New York: Oxford University Press, 2004.

Robinson, Eugene. *Disintegration: The Splintering of Black America*. New York: Anchor, 2011.

Robinson, Keith, and Angel Harris. *The Broken Compass: Parental Involvement with Children's Education*. Cambridge: Harvard University Press, 2014.

Rodgers, Daniel. *The Age of Fracture*. Cambridge: Belknap Press, 2012.

Roediger, David R. *The Wages of Whiteness: Race and the Making of the American Working Class*. London: Verso, 1999.

Roithmayer, Daria. *Reproducing Racism: How Everyday Choices Lock in White Advantage*. New York: New York University Press, 2014.

Rorty, Richard. *Achieving Our Country: Leftist Thought in the Twentieth Century*. Cambridge: Harvard University Press, 1998.

Ross, Howard J. *Everyday Bias: Identifying and Navigating Unconscious Judgments in Our Daily Lives*. Lanham, Md.: Rowman & Littlefield, 2014.

Ruggiero Greg, and Stuart Sahulka, eds. *The New American Crisis: Radical Analyses of the Problems Facing America Today*. New York: The New Press, 1995.

Ryan, Alan. *The Making of Modern Liberalism*. Princeton: Princeton University Press, 2012.

Ryan, Paul. *The Way Forward: Renewing the American Idea*. New York: Twelve, 2014.

Saramago, José. *Seeing*. New York: Harcourt, 2006.

Schacter, D. L., and E. Scarry, eds. *Memory, Brain, and Belief*. Cambridge: Harvard University Press, 2000.

Shapiro, Thomas M. *The Hidden Cost of Being African American: How*

Wealth Perpetuates Inequality. New York: Oxford University Press, 2004.

Sharkey, Patrick. *Stuck in Place: Urban Neighborhoods and the End of Progress Toward Racial Equality*. Chicago: University of Chicago Press, 2013.

Sharpe, Christina. *Monstrous Intimacies: Making Post-Slavery Subjects*. Durham, N.C.: Duke University Press, 2010.

Sharpley-Whiting, T., ed. *The Speech: Race and Barack Obama's "A More Perfect Union."* New York: Bloomsbury, 2009.

Shelby, Tommie. *We Who Are Dark: The Philosophical Foundations of Black Solidarity*. Cambridge: Harvard University Press, 2005.

Shipler, David. *The Working Poor: Invisible in America*. New York: Alfred Knopf, 2004.

Singh, Nikhil Pal. *Black Is a Country: Race and the Unfinished Struggle for Democracy*. Cambridge: Harvard University Press, 2004.

Steele, Shelby. *Shame: How America's Past Sins Have Polarized Our Country*. New York: Basic Books, 2015.

Stiglitz, Joseph E. *Freefall: America, Free Markets, and the Sinking of the World Economy*. New York: W. W. Norton & Company, 2010.

Stout, Jeffrey. *Blessed Are the Organized: Grassroots Democracy in America*. Princeton: Princeton University Press, 2010.

Sugrue, Thomas. *The Origins of the Urban Crisis: Race and Inequality in Postwar Detroit*. Princeton: Princeton University Press, 1996.

Thernstrom, Stephenson, and Abigail Thernstrom. *America in Black and White: One Nation Indivisible*. New York: Simon & Schuster, 1997.

Thompson III, J. Phillip. *Double Trouble: Black Mayors, Black Communities, and the Call for a Deep Democracy*. New York: Oxford University Press, 2006.

Tilly, Charles. *Durable Inequality*. Berkeley: University of California Press, 1998.

Tocqueville, Alexis de. *Democracy in America*. Translated by George Lawrence. New York: Harper & Row, 1966.

Tuch, Steven, and Jack Martin, eds. *Racial Attitudes in the 1990s*. Westport, Conn.: Praeger, 1997.

Tuck, Stephen. *We Ain't What We Ought to Be: The Black Freedom Stuggle from Emancipation to Obama*. Cambridge: Harvard University Press, 2010.

Tuveson, Ernest Lee. *The Redeemer Nation: The Idea of America's Millennial Role*. Chicago: University of Chicago Press, 1974.

Tyson, Karolyn. *Integration Interrupted: Tracking, Black Students, & Acting White After Brown*. New York: Oxford University Press, 2011.

Unequal Treatment: Confronting Racial and Ethnic Disparities in Health Care. Report for the Institute of Medicine of the National Academies. Washington, D.C., March 20, 2002.

Van Doren, Mark, ed. *The Portable Walt Whitman*. New York: Penguin, 1977.

Von Eschen, Penny. *Race Against Empire: Black Americans and Anti-Colonialism, 1937–1957*. Ithaca, N.Y.: Cornell University Press, 1997.

Walsh, Joan. *What's the Matter with White People? Why We Long for a Golden Age That Never Was*. New York: John Wiley & Sons, 2012.

Walton, Jonathan. *Watch This! The Ethics and Aesthetics of Black Televangelism*. New York: New York University Press, 2009.

Ward, Jason Morgan. *Defending White Democracy: The Making of a Segregationist Movement & the Remaking of Racial Politics, 1936–1965*. Chapel Hill: University of North Carolina Press, 2011.

Warren, Mark R. *Dry Bones Rattling: Community Building to Revitalize American Democracy*. Princeton: Princeton University Press, 2001.

West, Cornel. *Democracy Matters: Winning the Fight against Imperialism*. New York: Penguin, 2004.

———. *The Radical King*. Boston: Beacon Press, 2015.

Western, Bruce. *Punishment and Inequality in America*. New York: Russell Sage Foundation, 2006.

White, Walter. *A Man Called White: The Autobiography of Walter White*. Athens: University of Georgia Press, 1948.

Wilentz, Sean. *The Age of Reagan*. New York: Harper, 2008.

Williams, Juan. *Enough: The Phony Leaders, Dead-End Movements, and the Culture of Failure That Are Undermining Black America—And What We Can Do About It*. New York: Crown, 2006.

Wilson, William J. *When Work Disappears: The World of the New Urban Poor*. New York: Alfred Knopf, 1996.

Suggested Reading

Winant, Howard. *The New Politics of Race*. Minneapolis: University of Minnesota Press, 2004.

Wolin, Sheldon. *Democracy Inc.: Managed Democracy and the Specter of Inverted Totalitarianism*. Princeton: Princeton University Press, 2008.

———. *Tocqueville Between Two Worlds*. Princeton: Princeton University Press, 2001.

Woodward, C. Vann. *The Burden of Southern History*. Baton Rouge: Louisiana State University Press, 1968.

———. *The Strange Career of Jim Crow*. New York: Oxford University Press, 2002.

Wuthnow, Robert. *Loose Connections: Joining Together in America's Fragmented Communities*. Cambridge: Harvard University Press, 1998.

Yancy, George, and Janine Jones, eds. *Pursuing Trayvon Martin: Historical Contexts and Contemporary Manifestations of Racial Dynamics*. Lanham, Md.: Lexington Books, 2013.

Yoshino, Kenji. *Covering: The Hidden Assault on Civil Rights*. New York: Random House, 2007.

Zelizer, Julian E., and Bruce J. Schulman, eds. *Rightward Bound*. Cambridge: Harvard University Press, 2008.

ACKNOWLEDGMENTS

I have been undeservedly lucky to have the most amazing colleagues in the world. The faculty in the Department of African American Studies at Princeton is thoughtful, committed, and decent. Without them this book could not have been written. I am especially grateful to Imani Perry. The mistakes in this book are my own, but any insight was shaped and nurtured in my ongoing conversations with her. She read draft after draft and offered amazing feedback and encouragement. Naomi Murakawa read two decidedly different versions of the book. She pushed me, in her own gentle way, to be bolder. I have tried to follow her lead. Keeanga Yahmatta-Taylor also pushed me. She read two drafts and offered detailed commentary on each chapter. Her comments and criticisms guided me as I revised the manuscript. And Wendy Belcher, the master of all things, suggested the subtitle for the book.

I also want to thank my amazing research assistant, Matthew Claiborne. He found many of the people who populate this book. His work and care enabled their voices to be heard. I pray that I haven't gotten in the way.

A number of others were kind enough to read some version of the book or offered comments on a chapter: Kinohi Nishikawa, Stacey Sinclair, Ruha Benjamin, Joshua Guild, Michael Hanchard, Terrence Keel, Mayra Rivera, Daria Rothmayer, Daniel May, Kijan Maxam, Kevin Wolfe, Melvin Rogers, Jamal Calloway, Mark Jefferson, and Clifton Granby. Their comments and support helped me through some rough patches. Thanks also to the staff in African American Studies. April Peters, Dionne Worthy, Allison Bland, and Elio L. Lleo gave me the space to write and ensured that no administrative balls were dropped in the interim.

Acknowledgments

Thanks to my wife, Winnifred Brown-Glaude, for enduring my absences as I struggled with my ideas and with the writing. It is truly a gift to be wrapped in unconditional love as you're working. Her encouragement was boundless—as was her patience. Knowing when to give me space and when to force me to step away from the computer helped keep me sane throughout all of this. I am especially grateful to my son, Langston Glaude. While I was working on this book, he left for college. And I have been able to witness his transformation. He has always been amazing. What else could your only child be? But he has grown into a person deeply concerned about matters of justice. As his godfather would say, he is full of "prophetic fire!" And he inspires me daily.

Big shout-out to my golfing partners as well: Charlie Upshur, Larry Upshur, and Bob Langley. They insisted that I keep my feet firmly planted on the ground as I worked on this book (and relentlessly criticized my golf game).

I owe an enormous debt to my agent, Will Lippincott. He saw something in me and understood my aspirations. When we first met, I had no idea about how kind, thoughtful, and courageous he was. But that has become perfectly clear. I couldn't imagine having anyone else advocating for me and my vision of what it means to be a black intellectual in these dark times.

This book would not be what it is without the extraordinary care and attention given to it by the production team at Crown—especially Claire Potter and my editor, Kevin Doughten. I don't know how Kevin does it all. But he is an amazing editor. He *taught* me how to write this book. And, in this sense, the book is as much his as it is mine. I am thankful for his continued faith in me.

INDEX

Index

Black History Month, 95

#BlackLivesMatter movement, 66, 205, 209, 217, 224

black men, historical fear of, 76–77

Blackmon, Traci, 209

Black Panther Party, 86, 100, 150

Black Power movement, 90, 97–98, 123, 127, 150, 164, 166

Black Power: The Politics of Liberalism (Carmichael), 165

Black Twitter, 134

Black United Front, 169

Black Youth Project 100, 222, 233–34

Bland, Sandra, 6, 59, 201

blank-out campaign, 222–24, 232, 236

Blow, Charles, 221–22

Bond, Julian, 170

Booker, Cory, 151

Boyd, Leslie, 192

Bradley, Joseph P., 40–41

Braun, Carol Moseley, 166

Briggs, Cyril, 148

Brown, Michael, 4, 6, 29–30, 44–45, 59, 81, 128, 154, 179, 181, 187, 209, 212, 213, 214, 216, 219, 221, 225

Brown, Ron, 170

Brown University, 82

Brown v. Board of Education, 126, 149

Buie, Lucille Carr, 119

Bumpers, Eleanor, 201

Bunche, Ralph Johnson, 157

Bush, George H. W., 107

Bush, George W., 15–16, 107, 146–47

busing, 108

California, 97, 106

California, University of, San Diego, 112

Callahan, Leslie, 140

Calumet Heights (Chicago), 119–21

Campbell, Melanie, 173

cancer, 31

Carmichael, Stokely (Kwame Ture), 97, 165

Carruthers, Charlene, 222, 233–34

Carson, Ben, 154, 172

Carter, Jimmy, 7–8, 164

Car Wash, 139

Cathy's Kitchen Restaurant & Diner, 3–5, 216

Center for Responsible Lending, 16

Central Park jogger, 78

Central Reform Congregation, 209–10

Chaney, James, 104

Charleston, S.C., 128

Chenault, Kenneth, 124, 197

Chicago, Ill., 20–21, 22, 119–21

Chicago Anti-Eviction Campaign, 20

Chicago Defender, 134

Christian, Trayon, 58

"chunking," 56

Cicero, Ill., 96, 98, 100

citizenship, 31, 34, 126

civil disobedience, 215–16

Civil Rights Act of 1875, 40

Civil Rights Act of 1964, 40, 96, 179

Civil Rights Act of 1965, 105

Civil Rights Act of 1966, 96–97

civil rights movement, 18, 106, 108, 126, 127, 138, 149, 153, 170

according to Reagan, 104–5

Civil War, U.S., 40, 85, 102–3, 236

Clansman, The (Dixon), 76

Clark, Tom, 149

class, 122–23

class structure, 48

Clinton, Bill, 7–8, 110–15, 166, 170, 185

administration appointments of, 111

"initiative on race" of, 112

Clinton, Hillary, 171

Cohen, Richard, 73–74

Cold War, 149, 159, 162, 163

colonialism, 159

color-blindness, 103, 104, 107–8, 110, 157, 211

266

Index

Index

Index

Index

Index

Index

Index

Index

About the Author

EDDIE S. GLAUDE JR. is currently the chair of the Department of African American Studies and the William S. Tod Professor of Religion and African American Studies at Princeton University. His other books include *In a Shade of Blue: Pragmatism and the Politics of Black America* and *Exodus! Race, Religion, and Nation in Early 19th Century Black America*, winner of the Modern Language Association's William Sanders Scarborough Book Prize. He is a native of Moss Point, Mississippi, and a graduate of Morehouse College.